Also by Stephen Blewett

Practical Marketing and Sales
The 3D View: Business and Life Strategies
The 3D View: Living Your Successful Life Story

BEYOND THE LINE

Living an Active Faith

Stephen Blewett

WestBow
PRESS
A DIVISION OF THOMAS NELSON

WestBow Press books may be ordered through booksellers or by contacting:

WestBow Press
A Division of Thomas Nelson
1663 Liberty Drive
Bloomington, IN 47403
www.westbowpress.com
1-(866) 928-1240

Because of the dynamic nature of the Internet, any web addresses or links contained in this book may have changed since publication and may no longer be valid. The views expressed in this work are solely those of the author and do not necessarily reflect the views of the publisher, and the publisher hereby disclaims any responsibility for them.

Any people depicted in stock imagery provided by Thinkstock are models, and such images are being used for illustrative purposes only.

Certain stock imagery © Thinkstock.

ISBN: 978-1-4497-5198-2 (hc)
ISBN: 978-1-4497-5197-5 (sc)
ISBN: 978-1-4497-5196-8 (e)

Library of Congress Control Number: 2012908536

Printed in the United States of America

WestBow Press rev. date: 05/15/2012

Contents

All praise to our Heavenly Father and His Son, Jesus, who have given me more love than I deserve.

To Tracey, Chloe, and Caleb for always supporting me.

To my parents, who taught me to love Jesus from an early age.

To all the BTL examples I meet and see every day. You are all living proof of active faith.

Preface

The first-steps seeds for the writing of this book were planted when I was being interviewed by the editor of a large Christian publication. She was doing a profile piece on me based on a new book that I had just published in the secular market. Over the course of the interview she asked me the standard questions about my business accomplishments and previous published works. As we were wrapping up the interview, she caught me completely off guard by asking why I had never published a Christian book. It was one of those powerful God moments when you know that you are being prompted.

Soon after this, my career and life began to change. I felt the need to make some decisions. I was, however, afraid and searched for answers in Scripture. During this process I started to see the faith examples in Scripture in new and exciting ways. Their personalities, struggles, tears, joy, fear, and pain jumped off the pages. They became somehow real to me. These encounters with real people inspired me to make changes in my own life so as to demonstrate an active faith. As I journeyed through their lives, I was learning a great deal about myself. It was as if they were talking and teaching me through every trial and fear I was facing.

From this was born *Beyond the Line*. It was important that I made the characters come to life in the book, so I took the approach of an interview. This gave me the latitude to allow them to unpack what was behind the acts of faith we see them demonstrating. As I read and reread the scriptures through these God-gifted lenses, I noticed more and more exciting parallels and gems that I had never seen before. As I discussed these things with family and friends, I began to see examples of the living and active faith around me. It touched my life, and I stepped over some big, scary lines. I felt it was also important to document these journeys because it proved that BTL was just as active and real more than two thousand years ago!

What I hope to achieve with this book is to share in an exciting way how we can practically demonstrate our faith. My prayer is that you will be inspired and motivated to go further and grow in your spiritual journey.

Introduction

What is courage? Courage is in evidence when you step forward while others would step back.

"We are not of those who shrink back and are destroyed, but of those who believe and are saved" (Hebrews 10:39). Faith requires courage—courage to act. To move forward, you need to know where you are going and then take a deep breath and step forward . . . but not alone. When you choose to move out in faith, God steps forward with you.

In *Beyond the Line* we will take a journey of discovery. You will learn and be inspired by the wonderful examples in the Bible of people who weren't satisfied to take the easy path. When the opportunity to follow God in faith knocked on their door, they answered and followed. They stepped beyond the line! And their example challenges us to do the same today. But before we begin our journey together, let's spend some time examining your personal line.

Whether you recognize it yet or not, you have a line. You may not see it, but it is there. When you are a child, other people draw the line for you. As a teenager, you try to ignore the line. And as an adult, you fear the line. The line is real, and God expects you to step over it if you are going to grow. Not every line, but the one that keeps you from using the talents he has given you. God has mapped out a path for you. Each line is a step on the ladder to God. Each step is made especially for you and is always difficult to step over. But we must step over it, for it is only beyond the line (BTL) that we grow, learn, and get closer to our God. Be forewarned: you will feel uncomfortable when you move BTL! Maybe we need to feel uncomfortable, as this is when we are most aware of how much we *need* our God. This is when our faith is revealed. In the times when you feel out of control and lost, that is when faith becomes your GPS (God Positioning System).

Faith Is

The Bible is such a wonderfully crafted and inspired book. Hebrews 10:39 reads, "But we are not of those who shrink back and are destroyed, but of those who believe and are saved." This is the last verse before the "Hall of Faith" chapter, Hebrews 11. This verse is there to remind you of the courage we have through Christ to boldly cross over the invisible lines that threaten to hold us back. This verse is the BTL person's motto.

Many have gone before you who have set the example. These people in different ways have shown you how hard it is to step BTL but also what triumph waits for those who do. They also show us that faithful men and women have chosen to step over the line over and over again. Still others have been pushed over the line. God loves you and wants you to grow closer to Him. And yes, the line moves. Just as you begin to "master" the current step, another line will appear. You see them, but sometimes you will choose to ignore them and chart your own course. When you find yourself adrift in a sea of doubt and fear, then you will be tempted to blame God for not being there. Every day, Jesus watches the route we are taking as He wants us to follow in His steps and walk with Him BTL. However, knowing what step to take and which lines to cross requires that you understand where you are ultimately headed.

Faith is nothing without vision. Your vision must be clear. You need to see Jesus and truly want to be with him. He needs to be the one that keeps you centered and focused. He needs to be your plumb-line. The plumb-line was an instrument used in biblical times to measure verticals such as walls and fences. It was a string with a weight on one end, hung next to a wall to see if it was truly vertical. So who is keeping you centered? Is it Jesus? Or have you lost the one thing that keeps you focused? If the weight is cut from the string, you will be blown from side to side without any direction. Keep your life attached to Jesus, and you will be able to clearly see the lines that He wants you to cross. It is a simple measure. Hold the line up against your plumb-line-centered life and, if they match, then you are heading in the right direction; but if they do not, then question whether this is the line you are meant to cross.

"Do not conform any longer to the pattern of this world, but be transformed by the renewing of your mind. Then you will be able to test and approve what God's will is—his good, pleasing and perfect will" (Romans 12:2.) This passage is instructing you to transform your mind—in other words, to make Jesus your center and guide. Be careful not to rush in a particular direction without considering whether the path is laid out for you by God's will. Solomon gave us a warning with reading and rereading . . . *daily*. "A simple man believes anything, but a prudent man gives thought to his steps" (Proverbs 14:15).

What Line?

You may not see the line, but the truth is that most people are ruled by these invisible lines. Here is a practical example that I have used in many seminars and sermons. First you need to get some props—a bucket, three tennis balls, and some tape. Call three friends together, and ask them to each have a go at getting the ball into the bucket. Then in front of them pace out two or three large steps from the bucket, and place a strip of tape on the floor. What do you think happens? They will all have a throw from *behind* the line. We are so conditioned to act like this! The lesson is simple. You set out up-front that success was getting the ball into the bucket. They could have walked up and dropped it in, but they limited their opportunity for success by not going BTL.

It is true that some lines are wider than others, but every line needs to be crossed in order to step up to the next level.

Taking the Step

In August of 2009 I resigned as managing director of a major telco that I had run for seven years. I stepped BTL. It was not an easy decision but one I had felt for almost two years that I needed to make. I had tried to ignore the feeling. I had tried to justify why I needed to stay, but eventually I ran out of excuses. I had picked up the plumb-line in my trembling hands and could clearly see that the next step was firm and established. I was spending more and more time preaching and teaching and was not able to keep focused on my job. I needed to step away from something I was so comfortable with into an unknown next step.

To take this bold step required a practiced quietness. I listened for God. I could see the plumb-line matched up, but was this really what God wanted me to do? After some time of patient waiting, God's voice came through clearly in the common advice, opportunities, and support I received. I was reminded of these words in Isaiah: "Whether you turn to the right or to the left, your ears will hear a voice behind you, saying, 'This is the way; walk in it'" (Isaiah 30:21).

Let me assure you that you will go through feelings like those I had when I made this BTL decision. On my Facebook I wrote, "Today I have tears yet I'm smiling. I'm brave yet scared. I'm lost yet found, confused yet clear." Expect to go through these kinds of emotions as you go BTL. But, as we will see in the coming chapters, you are not alone. We all face the big BTL moments with doubt, fear, anger, joy, inspiration, and excitement. Above all you will find in the pages that follow ultimate joy and spiritual success for those who have gone BTL.

I was greatly encouraged by the definition of faith in Hebrews 11:1, "Now faith is being sure of what we hope for and certain of what we do not see." Faith is about spiritual vision. It is about making real what you have not seen. It is about being certain of Jesus and His love for us and strong desire to be with us. It is about confident courage.

Chapter 1

Noah — Captain, My Captain

John walks into the nondescript building and makes his way up the seventh floor. As the elevator ascends quietly, he forgets about the busy streets and honking horns outside. A faint *ting* reminds him that this is the floor. He has been invited to conduct interviews for a new magazine called *BTL (Beyond the Line)*. As he steps out of the lift, he is greeted by a woman with soft hazel eyes and a warm smile. She quickly ushers him from reception down a corridor to the interview room. She seems a little nervous and distracted as she offers him some water and bustles around the room checking that everything is just right.

He notices that the room has very simple furnishings and that it is set up to ensure relaxed dialogue. Two comfortable armchairs face each other with a small coffee table between them. It is apparent that this is about the discussion and not the décor. He settles himself into one of the chairs and takes out some notes from a faded and worn leather folder. He starts to peruse them carefully in preparation for the day's interviews. Just then there is a knock at the door, and a man with a boyish smile and twinkling eyes pops his head around the corner. "All set . . . er, John—or should I call you Apostle John?" asks Guy Kieser, the editor for *BTL*.

"John is fine. Yes, I am ready. Your assistant Rachel has been very helpful."

Rachel blushes and makes a hasty exit. Guy follows her down the corridor talking in excited tones. As silence settles in the room John bows his head in peaceful prayer to ask God's blessing on the day. He raises his head and glances at the clock on the wall. His first interview is about to begin.

Rachel shows the first guest in. He walks with a slight shuffle but steely determination. She quickly exits, closing the door behind her, and he takes a seat in the chair opposite John.

"Welcome, Noah, and thanks for joining me for this BTL interview."

"Thanks, John, it is pleasure to be here," Noah responds.

"Let's get straight into it," John says, "as I have so many questions to ask. To start with, can you describe for us what led up to you taking the BTL step of building a 450-foot ark?"

"Well, the short answer is, God asked, and I did. I suppose that often, when God reveals a future vision for us to fulfill, we pretend it didn't happen. I assure you I was shocked at the enormity of the request. God was not offering to build it. That was my task. He gave the plan, and I had to execute it. It was a big line to cross. The earth at that time was unbelievably lost. People had forgotten God, our Father and Creator. It was a corrupt and violent place. Everyone was just getting on with life. Parties, marriages, and business deals went on without God being considered or remembered. God was forgotten."

"Sounds familiar," John interjects. "Every generation successfully navigates further from our Father without even realizing it."

"Very true! I was chosen by God to step BTL. God knows what our talents are and will never give us a line we cannot cross. I found favor with God because I lived my life for him and not myself. He said that He chose me for three reasons: first, that I displayed righteousness; second, that even though it was such a wicked place, I had not slipped into the acts of the people around me; and finally, that I walked with God. The reality is that if your friend and companion is God, you will behave in a way that makes Him proud. To me BTL can also mean 'Be There, Lord,' as God was always with me whenever I stepped over the line."

"I read in Genesis 6:6 that 'the Lord was grieved that he had made man on the earth, and his heart was filled with pain.' These are strong words with a lot of emotion. Did you get a sense of this when talking with God?" John inquires.

Noah pauses and bows his head. Then he sighs and slowly looks up. His words are slow and deliberate, and tears well in his eyes. "Our heavenly Father loves us—more than I think we know and sometimes believe. His pain was raw and real. Every person is special to Him, and He wants nothing more than to see us inherit everlasting life. The big lesson for me was how far His grace extends. As I was building the ark, I kept thinking that I must be sure to have enough room for all of us and ultimately leave some space for grace. It was useful to think like that for the hundred years it took me to build the ark. The constant taunting, ridicule, mocking, and laughing made it tough. I knew that God could have built the ark in an instant, but because He loves all people, He was going to give them a lifetime to repent."

"A lifetime?" John interjects. "What do you mean by that?"

Noah smiles. "I am going to link a few thoughts now, all of which will help you in your BTL actions. The reason I say a lifetime is that due to the wickedness of people God had limited the lifespan of people to 120 years.[1] That's almost how long it took me to build the ark. People old enough to understand could have responded to the message. When you chat with Moses later, ask him to talk about the ages of the people who died in the wilderness for not wanting to go BTL with God. We all have our lifespan to choose life. The choice is ours. The people of that time, including friends and extended family, all had to take the first BTL step of accepting to walk with God. In the end only eight of us decided to do this."

"Fascinating! Even we forget that when we are called to step BTL, it often includes being an example to those around us to do the same." John glances at his notes and then asks, "Can you please now talk us though the whole 'flood experience'?"

Noah pauses as if reliving it and then responds. "Now that I had made a hundred-year BTL step, God was going to show His part. First, He brought the animals to me. I didn't go rounding them up. I thought that might turn some people's hearts, but all it resulted in was more mocking and some very unkind songs. I want your readers all to realize that going BTL for God is always going to be tough. The only way to keep going is to keep God beside you. Some people will think you are crazy. Anyway, God then shut the door with my sons, their wives, and my wife and me inside. We had three decks full of every kind of animals—and then nothing happened."

"Nothing!" John exclaims.

---

[1]   Genesis 6:3.

"Nothing. For seven days we waited. The door was shut by God, and the clock was ticking. People outside were now really having a field day. We could hear them jeering. I felt a mixture of anger and sadness. Finally, it happened. The rains came, and the water rose. I will not even begin to describe the sounds we then had to hear. Screams, pleading and begging . . . but God had shut the door. It was too late. If only people can see how easy it would have been. Just take the step, and you could have been saved."

"Isn't it true that people today also find it difficult to accept Jesus?" John adds, "A simple act that can save a life . . . your own!" Turning back to Noah, he asks, "What happened next?"

Noah continues. "It rained for forty days and nights. As you will recall, God *remembered* us. I never thought God would forget us, but I think the point is that, unlike all those who had forgotten God and drowned, God remembers those who go BTL for Him. However, it was not instant dry land and blossoms. We still had to stay on the ark for more than twelve months! I think this is a lesson worth learning for everyone responding to the calling God has for each one to go BTL. The act of going BTL is hard enough, but what is even harder is waiting: waiting to fulfill the ultimate purpose of this particular step. That requires patience."[2]

"It must have been a bit cramped on-board the ark," John says with a smile. "You must have rushed out of that boat and danced a jig of joy once the door opened and you stood on firm ground again."

"Actually, no," responds Noah. "We were overjoyed, but we needed to remember who had brought us safely to this point. It is easy for us to get caught up with the moment and think that we are the hero of the day. But we are not. The first thing I did was get back to building! I had built an ark, and now I built an altar to sacrifice and praise God for His deliverance. It was to be a permanent reminder of the grace of God."

"So how did God respond to this?" John queries.

Noah leans back in the couch and with a smile recounts the details. "He made some commitments. He promised not to ever destroy the earth by water again and that the patterns of the seasons would not be altered. He then said something so wonderful. He said 'Whenever the rainbow appears in the clouds, I will see it and remember the everlasting

---

[2]   Genesis 8:1.

covenant between God and all living creatures of every kind on the earth.' The emphasis was on Him remembering, but as you probably know, I was not expecting Him to forget. He is after all the creator. I think the point is that if a rainbow is a reminder for Him, surely it should be one for us."

Noah looks intently across at John "How many of us are still reminded of God's grace by the change of seasons and rainbows? How many of us in the joy, confusion, and action of BTL still remember what God has done for us personally? God has worked and will continue to work in our lives, and the signs are there—*if* we choose to look for them and remember them."

"So now that you were BTL, what was next?" John asks.

Noah shakes his head and smiles. "That very attitude is what can cause problems. God had instructed us to now go out and multiply. We had to produce fruit. Too often once people choose to follow God, they think, 'Well, that's it. I'm done!' In actual fact, things are only starting. You have completed the difficult part of crossing the line, but on this new step you have to fulfill all that God has planned for you. There is no retirement BTL. So that is what we did. We planted crops and had families."

"And became winemakers!" John interjects with a chuckle.

"Yes, we had a lovely cab that year. We called it Noah's Vineyard 'Faith Floats,'" Noah responds with a wry smile.

"Didn't you have some issues related to the wine?" John asks cautiously

Noah shifts uneasily on the couch. "I am sorry to say that we did. I did drink too much wine that day, and one of my sons acted foolishly because of it. What I learned from this is a vital lesson for anyone going BTL. When things seem to be working out just great, when the vision is becoming reality . . . be careful! A slip is so easy. It is the time when you need to be most vigilant while working and waiting for God to guide you to your next BTL action."[3]

After a brief pause, John concludes the interview. "Thanks, Noah, for joining me today to share your personal BTL journey."

John shakes hands with Noah and escorts him to the lift.

---

[3]   Genesis 9:21.

The 'Crazy' BTL

Not every BTL action you take will seem crazy. However, some might. You need to be careful that you are not making a move for the shock effect or because you feel you just want a change. Remember to keep praying, trusting, exploring, and *measuring* against the plumb-line of Jesus. You may not be called in your life to do something so crazy as to construct a boat miles from water. On the other hand you may have to do something that this present world thinks is crazy. You will know when it is right as I did when it came.

As mentioned in the preface, BTL was born out of some personal challenges that I faced. I was for seven years the managing director of a major telecommunications company. I had a job I enjoyed and people who supported me. Together, we produced stunning financial results over the years. While I was waiting for my next BTL moment, I was busy using the opportunity to make a difference in other people's lives on a public and personal level. I had already faced a few BTL moments before joining the telco company but none could even remotely be considered boat-building BTLs.

By my sixth year of work at the company, an uneasiness started to creep in. I couldn't quite place it at first, but then the signs and situations started to scream louder and louder. I resisted, ignored, and convinced myself that this could not be the next step. I eventually decided to share my feelings with some close Christian friends who, guided by Jesus, gave me their views—which fitted exactly with what I was sensing. The vision was clear. I needed to move out of the high-profile corporate environment and use my time to counsel, grow, motivate, and lead more people to Jesus using my own unique way.

I had already published a secular book that was creating the platform to teach. It was out of one of these opportunities that the idea for BTL was born. Like Noah, I realized that it would not be a quick BTL moment (some are!) but rather a process. So I quit my job after planning and prayer. *Everyone* in the industry thought I was crazy, but I had a boat to build.

I remembered the words of Jesus: "Suppose one of you wants to build a tower. Will he not first sit down and estimate the cost to see if he has enough money to complete it? For if he lays the foundation and is not able to finish it, everyone who sees it will ridicule him, saying, 'This fellow began to build and was not able to finish'" (Luke 14:28-30). Stepping BTL and failing causes people to ridicule not only you but—even worse—our Father. Just imagine if Noah hadn't planned how to build the ark and what resources were required. It would have justified the taunts. I knew I had to work, but what I could do was get a job that allowed me to still share what I knew God wanted me to share. The greatest blessing has been the number of opportunities that have suddenly arisen since the door of my boat was opened by God. Now it is up to me to produce the fruit!

I don't want you to be under the misconception that it has been easy. Any BTL act is a revealer. It reveals things about you, your direction, and those around you. The hardest aspect of this BTL act was the mocking, lies and attacks I had to endure. Some were expected, but others not. A fellow Christian I worked closely with turned away from me and distanced himself from me. He even went so far as spreading false rumors about me. I was, needless to say, hurt by this but in the end realized it was a small price to pay to follow our Master. I don't know why he responded that way, but maybe in some small way that I am not aware of, God is speaking through me to him.

As much as I had people who acted like this, I also had support from unexpected places and people. I love to imagine that every day as Noah arrived home after a tough day at the ark, his wife and family were there to keep his faith alive. I know that is true of my family!

So if you need to face your crazy BTL, just *remember* Noah—and smile!

Chapter 2

Abraham—Just Say When!

John settles back into his chair and once again prepares for his interview. Before long his guest arrives. He walks with purpose and confidence as he makes his way to the chair. He settles down and shakes hands with John.

"Good evening, Abraham. It is lovely to have you here today. Your examples of BTL acts are so many that we will just pick out a few. So as not to waste time, let's get right to it," John comments with a sense of urgency.

Abraham responds with a nod of his head. "Thanks, John, for the kind words. I'm ready when you are."

John smiles knowingly. "Your response right now just shows what I have read about your life. God asks and you do. It says in the Bible that 'Abraham believed God, and it was credited to him as righteousness, and he was called God's friend.[4] You see that a person is justified by what he does and not by faith alone.' What is it that made you so responsive to God's calls to go BTL?"

Abraham listens thoughtfully and then responds, "John, I think we must be careful not to assume too much. My first BTL test came when we were still living in Ur. I did not know God, and we worshipped other gods. In fact my father, Terah, was named after the god of the moon. My first call to leave Ur came, and I shared the vision and calling with my family.[5] They were very supportive. They were as motivated as I was to act now. So we packed up and said good-bye to family and friends and

---

[4]   James 2:23-24.

[5]   Acts 7:2-4.

set out for Canaan. That was our goal, our plan, our vision, and our BTL act. I will never forget leaving our hometown to follow the only true God. It was a big BTL step, and we were all filled with excitement and sadness. We were off to Canaan! But we didn't make it."[6]

"But you *did* make it!" John interjects, looking confused.

Abraham smiles and continues, "That's a common mistake most people make. We travelled 300 miles, following a route that stayed close to the river. To take the direct route across the desert would have been certain death. We arrived in Haran and stopped. Our intention had been good. Our zeal had been burning. By the time we reached Haran our BTL act had faltered. We had lost the momentum and ground to a halt. Life continued as normal, and we were successful in Haran. After a while the request of God was forgotten. What is important for you all to understand is that half a step is not BTL. BTL requires action *and* endurance.

"After my father died, the Lord spoke again to me with even more emphatic words. He said 'Leave your country, your people and your father's household and go to the land I will show you. I will make you into a great nation and I will bless you; I will make your name great, and you will be a blessing. I will bless those who bless you, and whoever curses you I will curse; and all peoples on earth will be blessed through you.' This was a specific BTL request. This time I was not only to leave my country but also my family. The blessings were sure, but I needed to make some sacrifices. If the family didn't want to take the step BTL, then I would. No more stopping. It was time to act. I was seventy-five years old when we left Haran for Canaan."

"You had a few problems after you got to Canaan?" John inquires.

"Yes, it was most definitely not all smooth sailing once we arrived in Canaan. There was a famine, and we went to Egypt to get food and had the whole issue with Pharaoh taking Sarah and my lie. Then Lot and I parted company because the land could not support both of us. It was a tough period of BTL. God had further kept encouraging me by saying that my offspring would inherit the land. I believed God but kept asking about an heir, as no heir had come through Sarah, even though God had said she would be the one who would give me an heir. You see I had *no*

---

[6]   Genesis 11:31.

doubt that God would do what He said. It was not *if* but rather *when*. When you take a bold BTL move, you need to keep focused and trust God to do the *how* His way."

"So was this when God changed your and Sarah's names?" John asks.

"At this same time God changed our names from Abram to Abraham and Sarai to Sarah. These names changes were not arbitrary but rather a further confirmation of God's covenant of promise to us, a reminder every day that we were living out the future in the present. Let's not forget that at this stage I was ninety-nine, and Sarah was ninety. We were no spring chickens, and it was difficult to keep believing that the BTL step had achieved its purpose. On top of this we had Lot problems again. Aren't family wonderful?!" Abraham allows himself the slightest grin.

"We had to negotiate his deliverance from the destruction of Sodom and Gomorrah. In our first 'incident,' I used my strength, but this time I needed God's grace. The reality is that God is gracious to those who believe and act on His BTL requests. He knows your pain and sees your patience. I had waited twenty-five years for Isaac to be born. I am still amazed that some people expect BTL acts to be revealed instantly. Part of the waiting is not because God is cruel but rather to refine and prepare us for the next step."

"You must have been thrilled at the birth of Isaac?" questions John.

"It was a day of such joy. It was the fulfillment of our faith. All the moves without knowing what was next were wrapped up in the little boy that I cradled in my arms. He gave us so much joy and was a living, breathing example of the promises of God being fulfilled. The BTL act seemed to be complete. Then it all changed. God was not finished with my BTL steps. God called and I responded. He asked me to take my son Isaac, whom I loved dearly, and sacrifice him. Of course I was upset and confused, but I had seen from experience that God was faithful to perform what he promised. As with all the other BTL acts, I was not sure *how* it would work out, but I knew it would."

Abraham takes a deep breath and continues. "It was tough. Very tough. We left early the next morning; I felt that, if God wanted me to do something, there was no reason to delay it. I had learned from our delay in Haran. Isaac and I left and together headed up the mountain. I want to share with you a private conversation we shared on the way up.

> Abraham took the wood for the burnt offering and placed it on his son Isaac, and he himself carried the fire and the knife. As the two of them went on together, Isaac spoke up and said to his father Abraham, "Father?"
>
> "Yes, my son?" Abraham replied.
>
> "The fire and wood are here," Isaac said, "but where is the lamb for the burnt offering?"
>
> Abraham answered, "God himself will provide the lamb for the burnt offering, my son." And the two of them went on together.[7]

"When Isaac asked me where the offering was, I could barely contain my grief. I had to believe that God had a reason and a plan. Often when we step BTL, we try to reason out what God should do rather than trusting that He will do what we need. When we reached the spot where God said I should sacrifice my son Isaac, I tied him up so that he didn't move as I sacrificed him. It was a powerful moment. He didn't run or resist. He trusted me and I trusted God. As I plunged the knife toward his body, I was overjoyed when God called my name. This time, even more than before. I was eager to stop and say, 'Here I am.'[8]. God had asked me to once again go BTL into the unknown with a plan that I didn't fully understand. I had taken the step, and our Father once again confirmed the great promise He has for all of us."

"In the beginning of our discussion we looked at how you were called the 'friend of God.' How does one earn a title like this?" John asks.

Abraham smiles. "God should be your friend also. You don't earn it; you act it. A friend is someone you trust, believe in, support, and grow to love. Friendship is cemented over time. If all of you are prepared to take the bold BTL moves with a clear vision, which sometimes looks far off, and still trust God, then you are also a friend of God. Ultimately it is about acting in faith. When God calls, the idea is not to be like Adam and try to hide. The way to act when God puts a BTL act before you is to shout, 'Here I am!'"

---

[7] Genesis 22:6-8.

[8] Genesis 22:1, 11.

John concludes, "Thanks for speaking with me, Abraham, and for your wonderful and inspiring BTL story. You are a true example that faith acts."

The 'Bold' BTL

I have had the privilege in my life to meet and interact with people who have displayed the boldness of Abraham in their BTL acts. Some of these people have given up careers and homes to do mission work in other countries. They have seen the vision, they have counted the costs and gone to unknown lands to preach the gospel. They are bold people with the fire of faith burning deep within them. The *how* is often not clear, but the direction is certain.

We are not all called to do this, but every BTL act is created especially for you. No one BTL act is better than another. I am sure the people who go on mission work would agree with this. It's just that this is their calling. They are called to live for Jesus and not for themselves. They are expected to give up the security of home to share the love of God with those in other lands. Ultimately they are fulfilling the promise that God made to Abraham thousands of years ago. "If you belong to Christ, then you are Abraham's seed, and heirs according to the promise."[9]

The reality is that you don't have to go on mission work to be bold like Abraham. You can be bold by standing up for Jesus. You can be bold by bringing more people to Jesus. You can fulfill your bold BTL by bringing more people to Jesus. It is so powerful to think that every time someone is brought to Christ, we are doing our part of fulfilling a promise that God made to Abraham over 2,000 years ago. In fact our boldness is Abraham's reward. Our faith is Abraham's promise.

I am ashamed to say that I have let so many opportunities to be bold for Jesus slip by. In my time in the corporate world I often let moments just slip by when it would have been so easy to be bold. This point was driven home to me by the simple act of an international sportsman. I had been invited to attend the gala dinner of this World Cup-winning team. A particular player was delegated to sit at each table. For the player it must have felt awkward. The rest of us all knew each other, and he

---

[9]   Galatians 3:29.

was the outsider. The dinner was a black tie affair accompanied by presentations, music, and a sumptuous dinner.

After the speeches and much excited chatting, the food was served. We were ravenous by now, and the food looked delicious. No sooner had the waiter delivered the plates than we all began to tuck in. Everyone except one person. I wish I could say that the person was me. It was not. It was the soccer star. He had bowed his head and was in quiet prayer. I watched as all eyes were fixed on him. After a short while he raised his head, smiled at everyone, and started to eat. This simple act changed the tone of conversation and attitude at our table. He had stepped out and revealed who it was he followed. He had revealed his faith. He did not know how this rowdy table of corporate executives would react. He didn't care. In the end he did what God expected of him.

You have been chosen to be bold. So, when the call comes, be ready to step forward and say, "Here I am. Send me!"[10]

---

[10]   Isaiah 6:8.

Chapter 3

Daniel — BTL in the Workplace

John settles back into his chair. He considers what an interesting and enlightening day it has already been. He is deep in thought when his next guest arrives. John knows he will give some interesting insights into how to go BTL in the workplace. He is what we would call a "high flyer" with his wisdom being identified at an early age.

He welcomes Daniel to the interview. Daniel walks in, and his presence can immediately be felt. He carries himself with confidence but not arrogance. He walks over and shakes hands with John, after which he sits down in an almost deliberate and calculated way.

"Daniel, thanks for joining me today," John begins, to which Daniel reacts with a nod and sheepish smile. "When I look at your life, there are many defining moments, but I thought that tonight we would focus on two BTL acts that we could gain great benefit from. The first BTL act I want to look at is your crisis BTL act with the great king of Babylon, Nebuchadnezzar. Please talk us through the events of that day."

"Thanks, John, no problem," Daniel responds. "I was taken into captivity in Babylon as a young man. The Babylonians were not only great warriors; they were also smart strategists. What they decided to do was to ensure that the most influential people of Jerusalem and Judah were put into the university of Babylon. Then the king ordered Ashpenaz, chief of his court officials, to bring in some of the Israelites from the royal family and the nobility—young men without any physical defect, handsome, showing aptitude for every kind of learning, well informed, quick to understand, and qualified to serve in the king's palace. He was to teach them the language and literature of the Babylonians. We were given Babylonian names, after the gods they worshipped, and mine was Belteshazzar. The schooling and name changes were subtle ways to get us to forget who we served while we worked for them."[11]

"That sounds familiar," John says. "So many people in the workplace are quick to forget that they bear the name of Jesus and His ways."

"You're right, John, but the influence is so subtle. Anyway, after a while we were introduced to King Nebuchadnezzar with our bachelor's in wisdom and understanding.[12] God had blessed us, and the king found us to be ten times more skilled than the rest of his officials.[13] With that in mind, we were destined for great things in Babylon Inc. We were on the fast track. But then everything changed."

"I assume you were shocked by how quickly things changed?" John asks.

"Oh yes! It took my breath away. As you said earlier, I was in a crisis BTL. A BTL step needed to be made and fast. King Nebuchadnezzar was disturbed by a dream he had but refused to tell any of his counselors the dream. Instead he wanted them to reveal the dream and then interpret it. The king was not known for his patience or willingness to negotiate and felt that his time was being wasted. With that he made the decision that *all* the wise men should be executed. This included me! When I heard of the order, I spoke to Arioch, the king's officer, and after some delicate negotiation, I convinced him to let me see the king. You must remember, by this stage the king was furious as he felt everyone was wasting his time and lying. It was a dangerous and stressful situation, as he could have executed his judgment right then and there. I had to take the BTL step in faith and trust that God would protect and guide me. I had declared that the living God would reveal and interpret the dream." Daniel stiffens as he considered the stress of that moment.

"God was with me, and the king gave me more time but not much. I realized I needed all the support I could get. The first thing I did was go to my friends and fellow believers, Hananiah, Mishael, and Azariah. I explained the BTL move I had made and the need for our collective prayer to God. I believe that often when we go BTL in a crisis, we forget

---

[11] Daniel 1:3-4.

[12] Daniel 1:17.

[13] Daniel 1:20.

to share the load. We need to have support in these moments." Daniel pauses for a moment.

"I want you to realize that God did not answer our prayer instantly. He reveals things in His time, not ours. Only that night did he reveal the meaning to me."

"I suppose you couldn't wait to tell King Nebuchadnezzar the interpretation," John interjects.

"Of course I was eager, but once again I would caution that in a crisis situation like this we need to think and *then* act. God had revealed the answer to make this a successful BTL act, and all praise needed to go to Him *before* I went to see the king.[14] I knew that once I revealed the dream and interpretation, King Nebuchadnezzar would apportion the honor to me, and I was right. I spent a lot of effort continually giving God the glory, but even with this the king heaped praise and honor on me. All of you who are ever called to go BTL in a very public crisis need to remember two things following a successful outcome. First, don't let it go to your head. God deserves the praise. Second, don't forget those who supported and prayed with you. They must also be part of the post-BTL success."[15]

Daniel slumps back in the couch after reliving the stress of the crisis BTL act.

John waits a few moments and then changes the topic. "Let's talk about your second BTL act. To me this BTL looks like it was born out of corporate jealousy."

"Yes, jealousy was a big part of it, but let me set the context. Literally overnight we had a reshuffle in leadership. Belshazzar of Babylon was out, and Darius of the Medes and Persians was in. It was a corporate takeover in the extreme. Everyone was nervous about their future, wealth, position, even their life. King Darius came in with a plan and started implementing his new structure from day one. He appointed 120 governors for the different regions, and above them he appointed three administrators, of which I was one. After a while King Darius decided, based on qualities he saw in me, to promote me to be over the entire kingdom.

---

[14]   Daniel 2:19.

[15]   Daniel 2:49.

"I have often observed that nonbelievers also recognize and reward godly behavior. Unfortunately, it does cause others to resent you. This is exactly what happened to me. The people who believed they deserved the position looked for every reason to catch me out but could not because my true boss was not the king but rather God. They eventually realized that they needed to attack me on something they hoped I would not back down on . . . my faith. With that in mind they used the law of the Medes and Persians and the ego of the king to get a decree issued that only he could be prayed to for the next thirty days, and offenders would be thrown to the lions."

John squints and asks, "But why did you need to go BTL in this case? It was only thirty days. You were going to be promoted into the highest position in the kingdom where you could do so much for God's exiled people. Why risk all that? All that was required was more discreet prayer for thirty days."

"Ahh," Daniel exclaims. "Now that is the problem with our fleshly minds. They are *very* convincing. I quickly realized two important principles. First, that my public and private worship of God must be consistent. Second, that I cannot let external circumstances change how I have always worshipped God. Faith is about consistent courage. That's the focus!"[16]

"It's interesting that you mention *consistent* courage," John excitedly remarks. "I noted in the Bible that when King Darius realized that he had been set up and couldn't change the decree, he mentioned the God whom you serve *continually*."[17]

"Yes, it is tough to be consistent, but we must," Daniel responds. "I was, however, not alone. God sent His angel to prevent the lions from killing me. This was an encouragement as well as a protection for me. God often does this once we are BTL. He did it for me, and He did it for Jesus.

"I want to make an important point about the purpose of this BTL act," Daniel continues.

"Sometimes we believe we understand why God does things, but we get it all wrong. The reason for this entire BTL act was not to get

---

[16]   Daniel 6:10.

[17]   Daniel 6:16, 20.

my enemies thrown into the lion's den but rather for God to reveal His glory to King Darius. I still get a thrill when I read the public confession of his faith in God: 'For he is the living God and he endures forever; his kingdom will not be destroyed, his dominion will never end. He rescues and he saves; he performs signs and wonders in the heavens and on the earth.'"[18]

"Well, I'm afraid that is all we have time for today. I sure would like to thank you, Daniel, for the wonderful insights into the BTL moments of crisis and challenge."

With this the interview ends and Daniel leaves.

You Did What?!

In my position as managing director of the telco company, I was expected to travel a fair bit. Most of these trips were mundane and uneventful. All except one.

I had caught a late afternoon flight to ensure that I arrived at my destination in time for a dinner with colleagues that night. As was my habit, I planned that I had enough time to check in to my hotel room and have a shower before dinner. Everything ran like clockwork. My room was ready and check in was easy. It had been a long week and I was very tired. I immediately unpacked my case and got ready for dinner. As I was about to leave, I realized that I needed to lock away my laptop in the safe in my room. That is when the night took an interesting turn . . .

I found the safe already locked, so I called maintenance, who came with a master key to open it. After much fiddling and muttering, the maintenance person managed to yank open the door. He then walked off leaving me to reset the code. It was then that I discovered that the safe was not empty. In fact, it was almost full. It was full with the equivalent of about $100,000 in *cash*!. I was stunned, and my heart raced. What had I stumbled upon? What must I do? After calming down, I eventually moved it to the hotel safe in reception to ensure its safety in order to hand it over to the management in the morning.

While trying to enjoy my dinner at a restaurant next to the hotel, I noticed a buzz of activity as very important looking people from the

---

18   Daniel 6:26-27.

hotel were in animated discussion. I approached them and asked them if they were looking for me. They denied they needed to speak to me, as by law I had not stolen anything but found the money. In fact they admitted later that if I had taken the money, they would have done nothing. In the end I was happy to give the money back, and they were relieved to return it to the previous guest.

So why do I tell you this story? Well, because of the reaction it received in the press. It dominated the media discussions and online forums the next day. I must admit to being somewhat surprised at the interest. It was then that I realized how we have become accustomed to politicians and businesspeople behaving in unethical ways. Even more disturbing was the number of people who would have taken the money, especially knowing that there would have been no apparent consequence. I am in no way suggesting I don't have many weaknesses, but in this particular BTL test I felt there was only one course. Most of the journalists asked me why I didn't take the money. In the end I learnt what Daniel knew. Our public proclamation *must* be consistent with our private actions. We can't have two lives. We are either faithful to God or not.

I pray every day that I will demonstrate consistent courage. I know that I often fail, but I am also encouraged by the lessons from BTLs like Daniel and the gracious love of Jesus that works in my life and yours.

Chapter 4

Moses — Preparing to Step

John welcomes his next guest. "Moses, thanks for coming in today, to help us address the concerns and questions we all have before going BTL. You have experienced a life that has made you a household name. You have been a slave, a prince, a shepherd, a leader, and a lawgiver."

Moses nods without saying anything.

John continues, "I have so much I want to ask you, but as usual we are limited by time. Since the theme of this interview is BTL, I would like to focus on one particular BTL calling you got—the call to deliver God's people from slavery in Egypt.

"In order for us to better understand this BTL act, I wonder if you could talk us though the circumstances that led up to your encounter with God at the burning bush on Mount Sinai."

Moses keeps a piercing gaze on John throughout this introduction. He seems to be absorbing and reflecting on all that is going on around him. When he speaks, he speaks with authority.

"John, I believe it is important to set the context of this major BTL act in my life.

"As many of your readers may be aware, I was born at a difficult time for us as a nation. Joseph was long forgotten, and we had become slaves in Egypt. I was born into very tough world. Pharaoh had decided to execute all newborn male children born to the Hebrews, which meant that I began life with a death sentence. However, my mother refused to accept this and hid me. After three months when I was being a bit too noisy to hide, she made another plan. She put me in a waterproof basket and asked my sister Miriam to watch me as it floated down the Nile River. Now that is a BTL act!"

A puzzled John interjects. "You speak very fondly of your mother. I am surprised, knowing your life story, that she had such a profound influence."

Moses seems a bit startled by the comment. "My mother was a woman of faith. Only a woman like that would believe that this baby had huge potential. Only a woman like that would put a basket into flowing waters and let God guide the path. Only a woman like that would ask my sister to be ready when God presented the opportunity for her to act. Only a woman like that could raise me for three years and at such a young age share her love for God and our people with me. Only a woman like that could give up her son to save his life and a multitude of people. Women like this are rare but powerful. You just need to look at Mary, the mother of Jesus, to understand what I am talking about. We must not underestimate the influence of a mother in a child's life!"

Moses seems moved by the words he has shared. He gathers himself and continues.

"Pharaoh's daughter adopted me as her own, and I spent most of the first forty years of my life in the palace. It was a life of luxury. I was a prince of Egypt, and no effort was spared to ensure my comfort and education. Stephen was correct in his assessment of that time when he said, 'Moses was educated in all the wisdom of the Egyptians and was powerful in speech and action.'[19] Those years were put in place by God to ensure that I was confident to speak up and—more important—to act. It was a time in my life that I would need to draw on at a later stage, but at the time its significance was lost on me.

"Then everything changed! I went to the defense of a fellow Israelite and killed an Egyptian bully. Before long, everyone including Pharaoh had heard about the incident, and I had to leave Egypt. It was a huge lesson for me. My willingness and desire to save God's people was going to be with His strength and on His terms. What I had thought was a brave BTL act was not supported by God. Yet I suppose that even when we make mistakes, God uses them to guide us.

"After this I fled to Midian. Midian was a hostile, hot, dusty and unforgiving place. It could not have been further from my life in Egypt. But isn't that how God works? He needs to prepare us for the BTL

---

[19] Acts 7:22.

acts He wants us to perform. I have realized that, the larger the act, the tougher and longer the preparation. At the time I felt confused and alone. Then I did it again. I rescued those who were being oppressed. This time it was a priest if Midian whose seven daughters came down to the well, where I was resting, to get water for their father's flocks. As they were about the draw water, some local shepherds chased them away, and I came to their rescue. That was the second such incident in just a short time"

"It's interesting you should mention that," John comments. "Now, thinking about it, I can see how the idea of rescuing plays out in your life. Your name means 'drawn out.' You were rescued from certain death on the Nile. You rescued a slave being beaten by the Egyptian slave driver. You rescued an entire nation from slavery. You rescued them from death by parting the Red Sea. The list goes on and on"

Moses smiles knowingly. "I didn't rescue anyone. God did! The first time I thought I could rescue anyone, I ended up being prevented from entering the Promised Land.

"As a result of my helping out the Midianite girls, they introduced me to their father, and I eventually married one of his daughters, Zipporah. Life seemed to have settled into a routine. I worked as a shepherd, tending the flock of my father-in-law. It was a simple yet tough life. I believe that sometimes God drives us into the desert to reflect, learn, and grow closer to Him. Isn't it true that when we are in adversity, we see God more clearly?"

John nods earnestly.

Moses then seems to change his tone of voice as if to underscore the importance of what he is about to share. "After forty years of wilderness preparation, God felt it was time to ask me to step BTL His way. I had taken the flock to Mount Sinai (Horeb) to find grazing, and as I was moving the sheep, I came upon a bush on fire, though it was not being consumed. This sight fascinated me.

"Then God called to me from within the bush. As did Abraham, I responded with 'Here I am.'[20] Unlike Abraham, I had doubts and questions. I was afraid of what God would expect me to do. I was willing to act, but God needed to understand my limitations. I was first told to

---

[20]   Exodus 3:4.

take off my sandals. The feeling of the sand beneath my feet somehow made the experience more real. Then God *introduced* Himself to me. He said, 'I am the God of your father, the God of Abraham, the God of Isaac and the God of Jacob.'[21] It was an introduction to remind me of the promises He had made to these great men of faith. I was afraid when I absorbed the magnitude of the moment.

"God then explained <u>why</u> He was talking to me. He felt compassion for His people and wanted to use me to rescue them. I was shocked, to say the least! So I resisted the request to go BTL. I questioned the choice of me as the person to do this.[22] I asked about whose authority I must appeal to for having been sent.[23] I spoke my doubts about my ability to convince the people of my authority.[24] I pleaded my limited talents and abilities.[25]

"Finally I came out with it—the real reason I was asking all the questions in front of that bush on God's mountain: 'O Lord, please send someone else to do it.'[26] I did not see the confidence that God had in me. The last eighty years of preparation seemed not enough. I was looking for reasons not to go BTL. In the end the most powerful part of this discussion is summarized in these words: "Then the Lord said to him, 'What is that in your hand?'"[27]

Moses pauses and John takes the opportunity to get clarity. "What is so significant about these words? You answered it at the time by saying that you had your staff in your hand."

Moses seems excited to share the paradigm shift that enables one to understand these words. "Yes, but that was not what was actually meant. When I queried the *how* of this BTL act, the Lord said to me, 'Who gave man his mouth? Who makes him deaf or mute? Who gives him sight or makes him blind? Is it not I, the Lord? Now go; I will help you speak and

---

[21] Exodus 3:6.

[22] Exodus 3:11.

[23] Exodus 3:13.

[24] Exodus 4:1.

[25] Exodus 4:10.

[26] Exodus 4:13.

[27] Exodus 4:2.

will teach you what to say.'[28] God knows our strengths. All He expects is that we use these unique gifts. If we do, no amount of doubting and questioning will prevent us from fulfilling the purpose God has planned for us. After I realized that, it was much easier for me to step BTL into a world that would make the forty years in the desert look like a walk in the park. God had used the desert years to ensure I was prepared for the big BTL step of leading His people to the Promised Land. In the forty years that followed, as we wandered in the wilderness, I often drew strength from the day that I spoke to God at the burning bush and was reminded that I had been prepared by God for this BTL act."

John seems at a loss for words and concludes the interview by saying, "Moses, I am humbled by the example of how God prepares us to step BTL. All He wants is for us to trust Him and act."

What Strengths?

I am still amazed that some people believe that they do not have any strengths. In the parable of the talents Jesus made it very clear that you have at least one talent and that you are expected to use it. Your talents are revealed throughout your life to ensure that, when you are expected to go BTL, you the confidence to do so. Moses became a great leader and friend of God once he accepted that God had a plan that He had prepared him for. God will not push us beyond what we can endure. All He expects is that we use what He gave us in the first place.

Your strengths are unique for the purpose God has for you. There are no grades of strengths. All that is required that you seek out your strengths. You may ask how we do this. It requires prayer, watching, and humility. It starts with prayer for God to help us understand what He has given us. It then involves watching for opportunities to reveal our strengths and humility to realize what we can't do and to take guidance and advice from those around us.

I love music and would love to play in the church band or sing on the stage, but it will never happen. I am not a skilled musician or singer. It does not stop my enjoyment of music, but it does mean that I must stick to the talents God has given me. What I have found is that when I

---

[28]   Exodus 4:11–12.

operate in my "talent zone," I feel charged and closer to Jesus so that I am drawn to operate there more and more often.

Don't try to reflect what you think your strengths should be; instead, exert yourself to discover them and use them. God will work around your weaknesses. Remember that when you enter the talent zone:

You add more.

You connect more.

You give more.

You feel more.

You are more.

As you consider God's preparation for you to go BTL, remind yourself of the journey you have taken. I believe that this is the reason that God asked Moses to take off his sandals. Yes, it was holy ground, but the feeling of the soil beneath his feet would have reminded him of the promise God had made to his ancestors Abraham, Isaac, and Jacob that their descendants would be as numerous as the sand grains on the seashore.

When I read this, I am reminded of a story I saw on TV of a rural man in Africa who visited some relatives in a vibrant modern city. He had grown up his entire life not wearing shoes with the African soil constantly between his toes. When he arrived in the city, his relatives were embarrassed by the fact that he did not have shoes, so they promptly bought him a pair. They were surprised to find that no sooner had they given him the shoes than he tried them on and took them straight off. Without a word he went outside and put a thin layer of sand in each shoe. He tried them on again and triumphantly declared that now they felt perfect. You see, for him the feeling of the soil was a connection to his past and his life.

So what connects you? Do you feel the connection of Jesus? Do you see the talents in your hand? If not, it is time to reflect on what has been done in your life, and allow yourself to be prepared for the BTL act God has in store for you.

Chapter 5

Rahab — The Unlikely Hero

John's next guest is a woman of character. She made a quick BTL decision that changed her life and the future of the world.

"Hello, Rahab, and welcome. As *BTL* is a magazine about action in faith, it is especially appropriate that we have you in the first edition. James says of you, 'Was not even Rahab the prostitute considered righteous for what she did when she gave lodging to the spies and sent them off in a different direction? As the body without the spirit is dead, so faith without deeds is dead.'[29] There are some important aspects to this description of you that I would like to unpack for our learning. First, how do you feel about being called Rahab *the prostitute*, and secondly, please talk us through your BTL act or deed."

John is nervous about the questions he has just asked, and for a moment it looks as if he has offended Rahab. Slowly she begins to smile as she ponders the questions and replies.

"Well, John, my reaction to your first question is yes. Yes, it is true that I was a prostitute. Yes, it is true that my life did not center on God. Yes, it is true that I was headed for a life with no hope. Yes, it is true that death was at the door. I don't ever try denying my past. I don't celebrate it, but I don't deny it. For me my past is a reminder of the grace of God, in that one BTL act was enough for God to forgive my past and bless me beyond even what I could imagine. Often the result of what we see as our small act is part of a big God plan."

"I assume you are talking about your family tree," John interjects.

---

29   James 2:25–26.

"Yes. My descendants included King David and ultimately Jesus. Isn't that *so* amazing? God does not look at our past when deciding on our future. He does, however, expect us to go BTL. I suppose that brings me to your second question, my BTL act"[30]

Rahab pauses as she takes a sip of water.

"We knew that Joshua and the nation of Israel were marching toward us, but we also thought that Jericho would be safe due to our fortified walls. The two 'spies' were not that secret. They had barely arrived, and the king already knew they were in the city and at my house. Things happened so quickly. I had already decided that these men were worshippers of the living God, but now I had to follow through on the decision. The true test of BTL is not the decision but the act itself. The spies had put their lives in my hands, and I in turn was in a situation that could cost me my life. If I had been caught, it would have meant certain death. I had chosen my direction, and now had to follow it through. This is an important point to remember when you go BTL. Once you have made the commitment, then there is no wavering or turning back.

"After I had sent the king's men in the wrong direction, I had a chance to talk to the two spies on the rooftop, where I had hidden them under some flax. I explained the reason why I had gone BTL. It was because I had heard of all the miracles God had done, and I now realized that He was the only true and living God. For me the motivation for going BTL is as important as the act. I still wonder why some people find it so difficult to go BTL even with so many things they have seen and heard. We all need to keep listening to ensure that we hear the message and are motivated to act."

"That's very true!" John comments. "Too many people see and hear what Jesus has done and still fail to be motivated to step away from past lives of hopelessness to go BTL for Him."

Rahab nods and continues. "Then I set up a verbal contract with the spies. I had gone BTL and wanted the assurance that my family and I would be protected when God destroyed the city. The lesson I learned BTL was that even once we have acted, we are still subject to rules and conditions. God will support and bless us for our BTL acts but we are expected to behave within the parameters he has set. In my case there

---

[30]   Matthew 1:5.

were two conditions attached to my salvation. First, only the people in the house with me would be saved; second, I had to leave a scarlet cord through the window I had let them escape through. These were not vague statements. It was a formal agreement between the spies and myself. God would deliver me only if I stuck to the terms laid out.

"I wonder how many people have thought about the two stipulations for my salvation and the implications for their BTL acts?

"Well, the first requirement was that I needed to bring my family into my home to save them. It was not enough just to tell them about what was happening. I had to go further. I had to convince and show them that they needed to follow my example and believe that they could be saved. We needed to support and believe in each other as the nation of Israel marched around and around the walls of Jericho. I needed to ensure that everyone kept motivated and focused because any attempt to leave the house would have meant certain death. Not surprisingly, some Christians still believe, when things get tough, that they must run away from the house and people of God. Strange, isn't it?

"The second requirement was that I leave a scarlet cord from my window on the wall of the city. Scarlet! Not brown or beige or gray but scarlet. Now that is a bold color. It is worth remembering that this cord was to hang out the window from the day the spies left. I was not to wait until I saw the nation of Israel at the city gates. I am not sure if you are aware, but that meant that I had it hanging out my window for almost two weeks before Joshua and the people arrived. The lesson from this is clear. When we choose to go BTL we cannot try to hide what we have done until it is convenient for us. We need to make it plain what and whom we stand for. We need to be obvious in our intent and reveal our support for God. How visible and bright are your BTL acts?"

"That's a very good point," John comments. "One of the first BTL acts many of us make is to come to Jesus. Like you, we walk away from death and into life. We sometimes, however, try to hide the act when the circumstances don't feel comfortable.

"So what was it like when the wall fell?" John inquires.

"What a day! Six days of trumpets and no talking and then everything happening at once. Shouting and the earth shaking as the wall crumbled. We were afraid, but no matter how many screams and calls we heard, we could not allow ourselves to disobey the commands we had been given. I cannot begin to explain the joy as our deliverers, the very same spies

I had helped, knocked on my door and personally took us safely out of the city. I was overjoyed that I had been able to save not only myself but those in my house. You see, we should not be selfish with the blessings of our BTL acts."

John once again interjects. "Yes, I read with interest that 'the young men who had done the spying went in and brought [you] out, [your] father and mother and brothers and all who belonged to' you.[31] The amazing thing is that not only had your BTL act and courage saved you, but your public demonstration of BTL had resulted in God seeing those with you as belonging to you. They were yours, and because of your love for them, God would show His grace to them. I am reminded of the prayer of our savior, Jesus Christ, to His Father 'I have revealed you to those whom you gave me out of the world. They were yours; you gave them to me and they have obeyed your word.'[32] We belonged to Jesus as His disciples. Not only us but also all people who choose to follow Him and obey the terms of our agreement as set out in the Bible.

"I think this would be a good place for us to wrap up our interview. I am sure that our readers will all agree that you have shown us that our individual BTL acts can save our own lives and be the basis for the salvation of those around us. All we need to do is have the courage to act and be bold enough to publically acknowledge why we acted."

Reach out and touch

The story of Rahab is powerful! No wonder it is listed in the examples of faith in Hebrews 11:31. What I find so encouraging is that when we act for God, he does not look at who you are but what you are. Unfortunately we look at external appearances, jobs, and status. The implication of this was driven home to me when I encountered a boy in Africa.

I was working in Mozambique on the east coast of Africa at the time. I had traveled with some colleagues to the coastal town of Beira. Mozambique, being one of the poorest counties in the world, had made

---

[31] Joshua 6:23.

[32] John 17:6.

me accustomed to seeing poverty and despair on a daily basis. But nothing prepared me for what happened that day.

We were in the streets of the city, going to a meeting. It was hot and dusty. Throngs of people weaved in between cars and along the busy sidewalks. In the midst of this chaos I noticed a boy about nine years old walking toward me. As he walked, his head was bowed with eyes fixed on the ground. People leaped out of his way as he neared them. I noticed, as he got closer, that he was so poor that he barely had clothes to cover his malnourished body. All over his body were sores. He obviously had nowhere to stay, and the way he looked repelled people. My heart bled that day. I tried to approach him to give him some money even though he was not begging. As I stepped in front of him, he looked up and in absolute terror ran from me. He was ashamed of himself and afraid of abuse. I followed him and eventually managed to show him I meant no harm. He finally put out a trembling, feeble hand and took the money I was offering.

I did not do enough!

To this day I pray for that boy in Mozambique. I should have given him more than money. I should have given him love—the love that Jesus gives me *every* day. Jesus showed how the Law of Moses that said "Do not touch" was not what was needed. He touched people with every disease. Jesus would have hugged that boy. He would not have seen the sores. He would have seen the broken heart. Instead, I chose to see the outward appearance.

I wonder if I could have trusted my life to a prostitute called Rahab.

Chapter 6

Gideon — Who, Me?

The next guest on the interview schedule is a hero: a deliverer, a leader, and a judge. John quickly seats Gideon as he is excited to learn more about him.

"Gideon, your BTL acts are legendary. I suppose that you are most often remembered for the defeat of the entire Midianite army with just three hundred men," John begins enthusiastically. "Please, can you talk us though this brave BTL act and any other BTL acts you may think are relevant for our discussion?"

Gideon speaks quietly but confidently as he responds.

"John, thanks for the kind words, but I would not call myself a hero. In fact I was initially afraid to act. I suppose I am an example of how God knows our unique weaknesses and works to ensure that we can overcome even the biggest doubts.

"When the angel appeared under the oak in Ophrah we had already had seven years of oppression at the hands of the Midianites and other invaders. The people were disheartened and afraid. We spent our lives in fear and hiding. That is why I was very surprised at the way the angel addressed me. He said, "The Lord is with you, mighty warrior."[33] I remember looking around to see if there was anyone else hiding in the winepress where I was threshing wheat so as to avoid the Midianites."

Gideon smiles and continues, "What 'mighty warrior'? I was hiding!

"My first reaction was to question. I felt a bit indignant. If this was the angel of God, then maybe he could explain why the great God I had

---

[33] Judges 6:12.

heard so much about had abandoned us. His answer was shocking and strange. He turned to me and said, 'Go in the strength you have and save Israel out of Midian's hand. Am I not sending you?'[34] First he could see in me what I could not. I was afraid to go BTL for Israel, but God knew what I could not see. He could see beyond my BTL fear. Victory would not be in the strength I would have but rather the strength I already had but was afraid to use. Secondly, it was a godly calling. If God calls, we need to respond. Often we ignore the call and make excuses.

"I was not only questioning but truly afraid. I really never saw myself as someone that God could work with. I was never a prince, like Moses, and my clan was very insignificant. Like some of you I felt that the wrong person had been called to go BTL."

"I suppose that's what the Lord meant," John says with a tinge of sadness, "when he told Paul that 'My grace is sufficient for you, for my power is made perfect in weakness.'"[35]

"Yes. It was a lesson that took me a while to learn. God's grace can compensate for our many weaknesses, making us ready and able to go BTL. Fear is not sufficient motivation to resist going BTL. This point was reinforced when the angel said that that I would not be facing the Midianites alone. God would be with me. No matter how lonely it feels BTL, we are *never* alone. Even though I had heard everything the angel said, my fear still needed more validation. Our gracious God knows our most intimate fears and failures and will work to ensure that we have what is needed to go BTL.

"For me it meant getting a sign. The angel gave me a sign by having fire come up from the rock and consume the offering I had made. It was a powerful example that God was with me on this BTL act. I was charged and ready to go. That same night God gave me the act he wanted me to perform. I was to pull down the altar to Baal and the Asherah pole and build an altar to God. I knew what I had to do but was still afraid. I refused to go alone. I brought ten men with me. I felt there would be safety in numbers. God would later turn my thinking upside down.

"The next day a hostile crowd was ready to kill me because I had destroyed their shrines. My father, Joash, managed to convince them

---

[34]   Judges 6:14.

[35]   2 Corinthians 12:9.

that if I had truly offended these false gods, then let them take their vengeance on me. It was a defining moment. I had firmly placed my allegiance with the living God, and there was no coming back from this BTL act.

"It was then that the Midianites, Amalekites, and other eastern people came to fight against us. I knew that I was called to once again go BTL for God, so I summoned forces from various tribes in Israel. Then it happened again. The dark, cold hand of doubt started gripping my heart and mind. Sometimes when we go BTL, hope is not the only thing that follows us. Fear and doubt stay in the shadows. So what did I do? This time I asked for not one sign but two signs. God knew my lack of trust and gave me signs. What a gracious God!

"Then God provided me with the lesson that would change my life forever. It started with 32,000 men gathering to fight the Midianites. God wanted me to stop relying in my own strength and rely on His strength. So he immediately made me whittle down the numbers. Those who were afraid to go to war were told to go home. I lost two-thirds of my army and was left with only 10,000. I thought to myself that even though this was a few, we could still prevail. But God had other ideas. Isn't it true that how we expect and even demand God to act for us BTL is not what actually happens? We must not forget that we step and God guides. It is, after all, His show!

"God then further whittled down the ten thousand to three hundred. All those who cupped water in their hands to drink were kept, while those who got on their knees to drink were sent home. I still believe there is more to this separation than we see. God wanted to send home those who found it so easy to bow on their knees to Baal. We may not understand why God asks us to do some things BTL, but His plan does have its reasons.

"By now I was very afraid. Only three hundred men! There was no way this was going to be Gideon's or Israel's victory. This was going to be God's victory. God once again understood my fears, and this time He guided me before I asked. I was told to go down quietly at night to the Midianite camp. There I heard some soldiers chatting, and they confirmed that God was going to give us victory. We managed to capitalize on their fears, and that very night they turned on each other. We started pursuing them, knowing that God had given us victory.

"Then came my next test. My own people started criticizing me and turning against me. When you go BTL, you need to overcome not only your own fears but those who refuse to help you. You will encounter those who believe your BTL act is not from God and are convinced you will not succeed. It is difficult to keep positive at such times, but we must. If we get drawn into this vortex of negativity, we will quickly descend to the realms of despair and anger.

"Ultimately this BTL act elevated my status in Israel. Now this is where the real danger lies. When we have successfully completed our BTL act, we can begin to believe that we achieved the success. Let me warn you that this type of thinking will only drive you to fail. We need to give the glory to God. My ability to go BTL was born out of faith that God was in control. Our deliverance was from God."

"It's interesting that you mention that," John comments, "because Isaiah says of your BTL act, 'As in the day of Midian's defeat, you have shattered the yoke that burdens them, the bar across their shoulders, the rod of their oppressor.' Your BTL act has become an example of deliverance."

Gideon nods gravely. "Deliverance from what? From our enemies? Yes, the Midianites were defeated. From our fears? Yes, my personal yoke was destroyed. I was set free from the fear that prevents us from going BTL. My faith was complete."

John's eyes light up as he hears these words. "I am reminded of the words of Paul to the church in Galatia: 'It is for freedom that Christ has set us free. Stand firm, then, and do not let yourselves be burdened again by a yoke of slavery.'[36] Jesus has taken off the yoke of the law and of fear. We need to be strong in our courage and free in our faith that He lives and works in our lives daily. We do not go BTL alone.

"Gideon, thanks for joining us and reminding us that fear is not a factor when we go BTL with God."

Trust

The story of Gideon may seem familiar because it is! In my own life I have experienced the following:

---

[36]   Galatians 5:1.

- God, you want me to do your will publicly. How about I do it secretly?
- Jesus, you want me to step forward and be counted for you. Are you sure this is the occasion?
- I am just one person. How can I make a difference?

If you have ever experienced these feelings, then you need to listen. Listen carefully. Can you hear it? It's faint but getting louder. Now it's screaming out to you. *My power is made perfect in your weakness!* Don't expect to be brimming over with confidence before you go BTL. Do expect Jesus to be with you! Trusting in this fact is important for BTL acts. I have often said to others that trust is earned, not demanded. Am I saying that God needs to earn our trust? No! What I am saying is that you trust those you have had experiences with and know. If you don't trust God, it may be because you have failed to recall what He has done in your life or maybe because your love for Him is waning.

There is an incredibly moving encounter with Jesus that I want to share with you. It is the story of the grieving father who brings his epileptic son to Jesus.

> A man in the crowd answered, "Teacher, I brought you my son, who is possessed by a spirit that has robbed him of speech. Whenever it seizes him, it throws him to the ground. He foams at the mouth, gnashes his teeth and becomes rigid. I asked your disciples to drive out the spirit, but they could not."
>
> "O unbelieving generation," Jesus replied, "how long shall I stay with you? How long shall I put up with you? Bring the boy to me."
>
> So they brought him. When the spirit saw Jesus, it immediately threw the boy into a convulsion. He fell to the ground and rolled around, foaming at the mouth.
>
> Jesus asked the boy's father, "How long has he been like this?"
>
> "From childhood," he answered. "It has often thrown him into fire or water to kill him. But if you can do anything, take pity on us and help us."

"'If you can'?" said Jesus. "Everything is possible for him who believes."[37]

Do you notice the path the father has taken to get to this moment with Jesus? He has tried the disciples and now full of doubt comes to Jesus. He really wants to have his son healed, but he just can't bring himself to trust in Jesus. In verse 23 Jesus makes it clear that belief is essential to ensure healing. Yes, it may not make sense. Yes, we may not understand it. But we must trust.

The most powerful part of this passage follows in verse 24, where the father's reply to Jesus' question should be our daily prayer when we step BTL in fear: "Immediately the boy's father exclaimed, 'I do believe; help me overcome my unbelief!'"

Trusting in God during trying times is when we are tested to the full. In June 2010 my seventy-four-year-old father-in-law was working in the loft of our farmhouse and fell. He ended up with severe brain trauma and was rushed to the hospital for immediate brain surgery. He ended up in ICU for over a month, during which time his heart stopped twice, and he was in a coma for most of it. The bills mounted, as he did not have the medical insurance to cover the costs. We had to make sure that he got the best medical attention and prayer support. Above all we had to trust in God. Then the miracles started pouring in! First, the neurosurgeon did not charge us for his fees. Loving people from across the world contributed to a fund we set up, and we covered his costs completely. He was discharged out of the hospital, and the doctors warned that he would have a slow recovery and require physiotherapy. Well they underestimated the love of our God!

Six months later, with no physio, he was walking and talking, and aside from a few small issues with recalling words, he is back to his old self. In fact, one of the first things he wanted to do was go back to church on Sunday. Being the faithful and stubborn farmer that he is, we let him go. When he went back to the hospital ten months after being discharged, the nurses cried to see him, and the doctor called him a walking miracle.

---

[37] Mark 9:17–23.

While we were on holiday with him recently, he revealed his own faith in a huge BTL moment. He explained to me how the nurses had asked him in ICU why he did not scream or weep like the other men in ICU. He lifted a feeble and shaking hand and pointed to the Bible laid beside his bed.

Chapter 7

Elijah—Hero to Zero

John looks directly at the guest in front of him and begins his introduction. "You've been called a prophet, a straight talker, and a true example of the essence of BTL. Elijah, thanks for joining me today."

John seems enthralled by the man seated in front of him and continues excitedly, "In reviewing your life, I found it so difficult to find what to focus on due to the many BTL acts you performed. So I thought that we would start with your first act of announcing the drought to King Ahab and see where that leads us."

"Hello, John, I am so pleased to be with you today" replies Elijah. "God called me to perform various BTL acts at a time when Israel had completely lost their way. They had chosen to replace the living God with a fake god called Baal. My first BTL act did not include much discussion. I was to deliver a message to King Ahab. I was to tell him that there would be a severe drought. The message was short and direct but it had some key aspects. I said to Ahab, 'As the Lord, the God of Israel, lives, whom I serve, there will be neither dew nor rain in the next few years except at my word.'[38] In one short sentence I had reminded Ahab that there was only one true God of Israel, that He lived, and that I served Him and no other gods or kings. Finally, all power rests with Him.

"I did the act, and then God told me to leave my home in Tishbe and go into hiding next to a brook in the Kerith Ravine. It was just northwest of my hometown, so it wasn't much of a journey. There I was to hide while God provided for my needs. The brook provided water,

---

[38]   1 Kings 17:1.

and every evening and morning the ravens brought me meat and bread. The lesson I learned from this initial BTL act was that God directs our steps BTL as He knows what we need. God knew how Ahab would react to my news, and He also would provide for me in ways I could never have imagined."

"It's very true," John interjects with a laugh, "that when we look BTL, we often fail to see a way that God can provide what we need. We limit God's power to what we logically believe can be done. Who would have thought of RFF . . . Raven Fast Foods?"

"Yes, we do see BTL based on what we think is possible and forget that *all* things are possible for the Creator of the world. This was a lesson I needed to learn.

"Anyway, after three years of drought and more miracles and moving, I was instructed to tell Ahab that the drought would break. Ahab, of course, was not happy to see me. He associated me with bad news. I explained that before the drought was broken, there needed to be a meeting of the people of Israel and the prophets of Baal on Mount Carmel. It was on the top of this mountain that I uttered these words, 'How long will you waver between two opinions? If the Lord is God, follow him; but if Baal is God, follow him.'[39] My BTL act that day was not only for me but a challenge to all of them. When we go BTL, we set an example to those around us. In my case it was to encourage the people to give up the apostasy, the falling away from God, that Jezebel, Ahab's wife, had introduced. Sometimes we are aware of the implications of out BTL acts, and sometimes not. Either way, the glory needs to go to God in the act fully accomplished, to ensure our example motivates others to act."

John says, "I suppose there was much debate and shouting after you posed this important question."

"Actually, no," Elijah responds. "There was dead silence. The people said nothing. Even today when people are asked to choose God or the world's ways, they choose to ignore the question.

"I knew the act needed to be big to show a big and living God. My suggestion, which was accepted, was that two bulls were to be cut in pieces and placed on some wood. One was to be placed on the altar of

---

[39] 1 Kings 18:21.

Baal and the other on my altar. They were not to be set alight by human hands. I let the 450 prophets of Baal go first. They prepared the sacrifice as agreed and spent the entire morning dancing and calling out to Baal. By noon I was a bit bored and irritated. I threw in a few choice jibes. 'Shout louder!' I said. 'Surely he is a god! Perhaps he is deep in thought, or busy, or traveling. Maybe he is sleeping and must be awakened.'[40] This made them even madder. They shouted louder, yelling themselves hoarse, and began cutting themselves until the blood flowed. Isn't it amazing how those who refuse to believe will do *anything* to prove they are right?

"By the evening I decided it was time to act. I first repaired the altar of the Lord. I took twelve stones, to represent the twelve tribes of Israel, to use in the repairs. Often doing this kind of thing makes people part of the BTL act we perform. We should try making our BTL acts inclusive rather than exclusive. Then I dug a trench around the altar and asked that four large jars of water be poured over the offering and the wood three times! This made the entire area wet and impossible to set afire with human hands. Using so much water also drove home my faith that God would stop the drought.

"I prayed to God, and He answered. He sent fire that consumed the sacrifice, the wood, and the water in the trenches. It was a fantastic display of the awesome power of our God! Of course now the people started shouting 'The Lord—he is God! The Lord—he is God!'[41] Funny how people often need to see to believe. Well, I was relieved that they had come with me BTL, and now I needed them to demonstrate that. I asked them to capture the prophets of Baal, and we killed them all that day in the Kishon valley below.

I went back up Mount Carmel for some reflection and prayer. Sometimes in the frenzied activity of BTL, we forget to go back and thank God. I needed to do this and also to wait for the Lord to break the drought. It was late that evening that eventually the clouds began to build and God sent heavy rains. I cannot explain the joy of feeling the rain against my face for the first time in three years!"

"But how did you go from the euphoria to despair so quickly?" John asks cautiously

---

[40]   1 Kings 18:27.

[41]   1 Kings 18:39.

Elijah stares into nothingness and then turns to John and says, "Because I forgot God.

"When you have made such a public BTL move and have been revealed as a hero for God, then be warned that your greatest test will come in living up to what you have taught and acted on. BTL is not one act. It is part of a process in growing our faith. God will test us to ensure that our BTL act is life changing rather than a momentary demonstration of courage. It needs to be continuous and consistent to be effective.

"For me that challenge came with the threat from Jezebel that within twenty-four hours she would kill me. I hit an all-time low and ran. I ran from her. I ran from my responsibilities. I ran for my life. I got as far south as Beersheba and left my servant there. I then went on alone. I was in deep depression and felt that this was it. I had done enough. My BTL acts were large and challenging, and I was drained. I did not need or want any more challenges. This kind of thinking is common at different stages in our lives when we feel drained after going BTL over and over again. We just want to give up, and I did. I 'went a day's journey into the desert. I came to a broom tree, sat down under it and prayed' that I might die. 'I have had enough, Lord,' I said. 'Take my life; I am no better than my ancestors.'[42] My plan was to go far down south to Mount Sinai (Horeb) to hide from Jezebel. But I only managed to travel one day and fall asleep out of mental and physical exhaustion under a broom tree. I was ready to die, but God was not ready to let me give up. He sent his angel twice to feed me twice. What I noticed was that the food was a reminder. The bread was the same type the ravens had fed me with, and the jar of water was a reminder of God's mighty power on Mount Carmel."

"That's amazing, how God puts little clues in our lives BTL," John notes. "We need to look for these clues in our darkest hours."

"Yes, they are there if we take the time to look for them," Elijah confirms. "It worked for me. I was now ready to continue my journey to the Lord's mountain. It took me forty days and nights to get to Mount Sinai."

---

[42]   1 Kings 19:4.

"This forty days and nights seems significant," John says, "if you consider that Moses spent forty days and nights getting the commandments on that very same mountain, and Jesus spent forty days and nights fasting in the desert when he was tempted. Your forty days and nights traveling almost seem like a bridge between the two events as you traveled through the *desert* to get to *Mount Sinai.*"

John's words trail off as he suddenly realizes something. He looks at Elijah and says, "That was why you were there. Wasn't it?"

John composes himself and explains. "Let me share what happened to me. After six days Jesus took Peter, James and myself with him and led us up a high mountain, where we were all alone. There he was transfigured before us. His clothes became dazzling white, whiter than anyone in the world could bleach them. And there appeared before us Elijah and Moses, who were talking with Jesus.[43] Two significant BTL men of faith were with Jesus to encourage him to never give up."

Elijah smiles knowingly and continues, "Yes, we all go through our tests and trials, but in the end it's not the journey but the destination that counts. I had arrived at Mount Sinai and did what I thought was best: I hid in a cave. Then God appeared to me and asked me what I was doing hiding on Mount Sinai, miles away from the people whose hearts I was meant to be turning back to Him. I of course explained that I was all alone, and the people did not want to listen even with great signs and wonders. Then I had a life-changing experience. 'The Lord said, "Go out and stand on the mountain in the presence of the Lord, for the Lord is about to pass by." Then a great and powerful wind tore the mountains apart and shattered the rocks before the Lord, but the Lord was not in the wind. After the wind there was an earthquake, but the Lord was not in the earthquake. After the earthquake came a fire, but the Lord was not in the fire. And after the fire came a gentle whisper.'[44]

"That whisper was what drew me to the entrance of the cave. All the great, powerful acts of wind, earthquake, and fire where terrifying but not revealing. God is in the message, not the act. God is guiding, not performing. God speaks. All we need to do is listen and act for Him. I was so busy condemning the people for their lack of response to the

---

[43]   Mark 9:2-4.

[44]   1 Kings 19:11-12.

mighty acts that I had failed to see and hear that I was not alone. Seven thousand people were not following Baal. I was not alone. I was never alone. I had heard the gentle whisper and I was comforted."

"I think our readers will all agree that we are comforted by your words tonight. You have shown us that even when we perform the big BTL acts, the real value is in the message and not the act. May we all strive to listen carefully for the gentle guidance of the whisper of God."

The Vow of Quietness

I recently heard someone say that wisdom is the right application of knowledge. The events of Elijah's life are full of wisdom. The true value is what you take out of the knowledge you have gained for personal, practical application. For me, the lesson from Elijah is one that I wish I had listened for a long time ago. Almost without fail I have fallen into the trap of getting overexcited about the act itself and not the message it delivers. I have got caught up in BTL successes in my life and become self-centered rather than God-centered. Then when the first adversity happens, I am ready to throw in the towel as all the energy is sucked out of me.

Then I read the following words in Ecclesiastes: there is "a time to tear and a time to mend, a time to be silent and a time to speak."[45] There was the answer I was looking for. Do you see it? A better question is, Do you hear it? When we are so busy doing, we fail to see the message. I have found it invaluable to commit to a Vow of Quietness. It is a personal commitment to speak far less than I normally would. (Anyone who knows me will tell you this is a real challenge!) It is a way of allowing your BTL moment to act on you and spread to those around you. It is a way of allowing the gentle whisper of God to speak to you. You will find that it opens up a whole new world in the midst of the activity and attention of your large public BTL acts. Like Elijah you will not feel alone. You will start to see how God is working through and with you to call more and more people to Him. In your quietness your BTL acts shout the loudest.

---

[45] Ecclesiastes 3:7.

I would also suggest to you that there is another aspect to the voice Elijah heard that we must not lose sight of. It was after all a *gentle* whisper. For me this speaks of the comforting nature of our Father. This could also be called love. In Jesus we see and hear the gentle whisper clearly. He refused to be drawn into huge demonstrations of His obvious power. Instead He chose to change people's hearts one touch, one lesson, and one miracle at a time. He chose to use the gentle whisper of love to overcome the hate of the world. But were they listening? Are you listening now?

"I tell you the truth, whoever hears my word and believes him who sent me has eternal life and will not be condemned; he has crossed over from death to life."[46]

---

[46] John 5:24.

Chapter 8

David — The Heart of God

"You have been called a man after God's own heart and lie in the direct line of Jesus. You are a man of passion that we can all identify with. Welcome, David!

"Thanks so very much for joining me today. What an honor and a privilege for me to be able to hear you share some of your BTL moments. Obviously, in your case in particular, we can't cover all your BTL acts. I must admit to being surprised at some of the parts of your life you chose for us to discuss. But rather than spoil the surprise, let me hand it over to you."

David's voice is gentle yet commanding as he responds. "Thanks, John. As you mentioned, I do have BTL moments that may surprise some people. I would, however, prefer to be real in the way I present myself and to also allow others to learn, prepare, and act on the appropriate BTL moments that are placed before them.

"The first BTL act I want to review with you is the one you are most familiar with. For me it set the tone for the rest of my life. I would face many 'giants' in my life. Some I would defeat, and some would defeat me. The result might have varied in these BTL acts, but the lesson was consistent. We all face giant moments in our lives. Some are obvious hairy nine-foot-tall moments that we take head-on and overcome. Others start off small and end up towering over us as we weep in the knowledge that we failed. We all face the elation and despair in our personal BTL challenges. Don't expect to be victorious every time, but do expect to keep trying.

"So let me start with my first major public BTL moment. The events leading up to the moment I faced Goliath were the culmination of several converging developments. The prophet Samuel had anointed me to be the next king of Israel. Saul, not knowing this, had asked for me to play the harp to soothe his raging temper. Amid all this I was still tending my father's flocks while three of my brothers went out to war against the Philistines with King Saul. It was in this context that God called me to finally step BTL publically.

"My now aged father asked me to deliver some supplies to my brothers, who had already been facing the Philistines for forty days. Both sides were not yet prepared to engage in full scale warfare, so instead, every day, they drew up battle lines facing each other. Then Goliath would come out and taunt the army of King Saul, saying, 'Why do you come out and line up for battle? Am I not a Philistine, and are you not the servants of Saul? Choose a man and have him come down to me. If he is able to fight and kill me, we will become your subjects; but if I overcome him and kill him, you will become our subjects and serve us.' Then the Philistine said, 'This day I defy the ranks of Israel! Give me a man and let us fight each other.'[47]

"I left early in the morning to deliver the supplies and arrived as Goliath was performing his daily ritual. I saw the fear, terror, and dismay of the army as Goliath spoke. I felt their anguish, and my heart burned with indignation. This mere mortal was mocking the living God—the God who had guided me as I killed the lion and bear that attacked my father's flock, the God whose presence surrounded me in the plains and mountains as the sheep grazed. I could have felt that all the time I spent protecting and watching the sheep was wasted. But it wasn't. God was using it to prepare me for my BTL act."

Looking intently at John, he continues: "Consider your own life, and be careful not to assume that you are going nowhere. Remember that God never forgets us, and as people read this, He is preparing them for their next step BTL. I know this was true for me.

"I started excitedly asking why this man was allowed to defy the living God. My oldest brother, Eliab, heard me talking to the men and angrily attacked me. 'Why have you come down here? And with whom

---

[47] 1 Samuel 17:8–10.

did you leave those few sheep in the desert? I know how conceited you are and how wicked your heart is; you came down only to watch the battle.' You will all find that when you feel moved by God to go BTL, there will always be those, sometimes even close family, who will attack you and attempt to destroy your passion and drive. We can't hope to convince these people to support us, so we simply have to ignore them and move past them.

"By now King Saul knew of my desire to fight this Philistine. He attempted to support me by giving me his armor to face Goliath. I tried it on, but it did not work for me. Here too is a lesson for you when you go BTL. If support is offered, embrace it. Then try it on for size, and if it does not work for you or help you go BTL, then respectfully decline it. So I stayed with what had worked for me and felt comfortable. I kept my simple tunic, took my shepherd's staff and sling, and went down to the river to select five smooth stones. You must remember that the river ran in the valley as a natural divider with both armies on opposing hills. All eyes were trained on me as I went about the business of selecting my stones. I knelt on the green grass at the river's edge as a young shepherd boy with a staff in my hand. I saw the giant Goliath towering over me in the distance, and I remembered that God had sent Samuel to anoint me to fight for Him. Amid the chaos and clamor I quietly prayed these words, and many of them resonated deeply in my soul.

> The Lord is my shepherd, I shall not be in want.
> He makes me lie down in *green pastures*, he leads me *beside quiet waters*,
> he restores my soul. He guides me in paths of righteousness for his name's sake.
> Even though I walk through the *valley* of the *shadow of death*, I will fear no evil, for you are with me; your rod and your *staff*, they comfort me.
> You prepare a table before me in the presence of *my enemies*.
> You *anoint my head* with oil; my cup overflows.
> Surely goodness and love will follow me all the days of my life, and I will dwell in the house of the Lord forever.[48]

---

[48] Psalm 23.

When I stood up, I was ready to face my giant with confidence. I knew that no matter how big and menacing Goliath looked, God had bigger and better BTL acts he still wanted me to perform. I saw BTL.

"Don't ever, ever, ever forget what I have just said. When the act seems huge, *see BTL*. Your act is part of bigger and better things that have been planned just for you. It's called vision, and you need to keep it before, after, and during BTL."

"Please tell me about the time you didn't go BTL," John prompts, "although all the signs seemed to indicate that you should act."

"I assume you are talking about when King Saul, in his crazed fit of jealousy, was hunting me all over Israel and happened to go into a cave to relieve himself. Of all the caves in all Israel, he happened to come unarmed into the one that we were hiding in. Outside were his three thousand men. Inside the cave we far outnumbered the solitary king. It was dark and a perfect opportunity to kill him. My men urged me to kill him, but instead I just cut off the edge of his robe. He didn't even notice, but it still made me feel guilty. This was my master and God's first king of Israel. How could I even think of disrespecting him in this way? This was not the BTL act that God wanted me to take. God would deliver the kingdom to me in his time and on his terms.

"Once again there are lessons for you. First, be careful that you don't try justifying in your mind that something seems so obvious even when you know in your heart it is wrong. Secondly, always think, pray, and test before you act on any BTL challenge. Don't set the agenda and timing for your spiritual growth. That's God's job."

"It's so tricky to know what is a required BTL act as opposed to a false BTL act," John comments. I agree we need to be cautious. Have you ever gone BTL on the wrong act?"

David smiles and nods. "Of course. I am, as you all know, not perfect. I made some huge mistakes by crossing some lines I should never have crossed. They were BTL acts I should have avoided. One that sticks out the most was my affair with Bathsheba and the subsequent murder of Uriah."

David draws a deep breath and continues: "I simply let my guard down. I had allowed myself to drift from being active for God. I was taking a break on the step of my BTL growth. Before I knew it, I was justifying and stepping over lines that God had not drawn. When Nathan the prophet came to see me and presented me with a story of a rich man lording it over and abusing his poor neighbor, I was very angry. I was ready to kill the unscrupulous, callous rich man. Then Nathan said some words I will never forget. 'You are the man!'[49] I had condemned myself. I was the man who had stepped BTL where I should not. I was the man who had failed God. I was the man." With that his voice trails off.

Then David continues, now quieter and subdued. "There were consequences because of my actions. Stepping BTL where we should not always results in hurt and pain. Some lines are left well alone. Don't even try looking or getting close to these lines. They are dangerous. However, even though I did not deserve it, God took away this sin and forgave me. The lesson is clear. Don't cross lines you know you should avoid. If you do, you will suffer, but always remember that you can find your way back if you truly repent and start once again looking for the BTL acts God wants you to perform."

John quietly concludes the interview by thanking David for joining him.

Choose Carefully

The interview with David highlights three types of BTLs. First, BTLs that are big and scary that obviously must be faced and overcome. Second, BTL'=s that you convince yourself are required and supported by God. Third, BTLs that are plain wrong and you know it!

You have spent some time already looking at the first type of BTL act. I would like to spend some time reflecting on types two and three.

BTLs that you convince yourself God supports are common. I am sure you have experienced your fair share. I would like to share one such occasion for our common learning. Many years back, as a young married couple, we were living in a vibrant city and actively involved in the church. I, however, secretly yearned for more challenges and career growth. The multinational company I worked for presented me with an opportunity to move to a different country. My wife, Tracey, did not like the idea, and after we visited the country, she was even less convinced. On the other hand, I really liked the opportunity for growth and of course the money. I spent hours convincing Tracey, family, friends, and

---

[49]   2 Samuel 12:7.

ultimately myself that this was a big BTL step that God wanted us to take. We were going to do mission work and grow in our relationship, etc. You get the idea! Well, we went—and it was a huge disaster. The job was terrible, my wife got very sick and had to return home, my faith declined, and I sat all alone in a foreign country. I will never forget one Saturday night kneeling at the foot of my bed and begging God to forgive me for my foolishness. He did, and I was soon transferred back home to a better position that allowed me to grow His way.

As an interesting aside, five years later we went back to that same country. This time God set the challenge, and the signs were obvious. Everything just fell into place before and after we went BTL. I can with all confidence tell you that I would rather go BTL when God calls.

The third type of BTL should glow *red*! I cannot believe how many people flirt with lines that should not be crossed. They approach these lines in the full confidence that they can handle it—that they will get close but won't cross, that they will only stand and look to the other side. Let's not be foolish to believe that we won't commit adultery, look at porn, take drugs, drink too much . . . the list goes on and on.

I think it would be fitting for David to have the last word. In Psalm 1:1 he describes the progression down the slippery slope of sin. The warning is simple. Don't even go down that road. This is *not* a BTL you should even think about.

> Blessed is the man who does not *walk* in the counsel of the wicked or *stand* in the way of sinners or *sit* in the seat of mockers.

Chapter 9

Jonah — Anyone for Fish?

" There is no doubt that my next guest serves God and is zealous in his commitment to the people of God. He prophesied during the reign of King Jeroboam II of Israel."

Jonah smiles. His inquisitive, twinkling eyes soften his tough exterior.

"Jonah, thanks for joining me today. I hope the journey here was without incident?" John asks, tongue in cheek.

"No problems," Jonah answers with a chuckle. "It was clear sailing. Nothing swallowed me this time. Although you never know about the way back!"

"Jonah, how about if you share with us what led up to you having to go BTL at God's instruction and what we can all learn from it."

Jonah pauses as if recalling the facts and then begins. "As you say, I was a prophet during the time of King Jeroboam II. I had spent most of my life warning the people of Israel to change their ways or the Assyrians would bring them into captivity. The capital city of Assyria at this time was Nineveh. Then I got this message from God: 'Go to the great city of Nineveh and preach against it, because its wickedness has come up before me.'[50] Imagine my shock, dismay, and despair on hearing this. God was asking me to preach in this evil Gentile city, that *I had foretold* would treat my own people cruelly. I could not see any logical reason to help them. They were the enemy. Why should I go BTL for them?"

"That sounds familiar!" John adds. "Often we ask *why me* and *why them?*"

---

[50]   Jonah 1:2.

"Well put," Jonah responds. "I had decided not to take up the challenge. I lived in a town called Gath Hepher a hundred miles north of Jerusalem[51] and headed for the coastal town of Joppa. Joppa was close to Jerusalem and served the needs of the city. I had decided to get as far away from Nineveh as possible, so I boarded a ship for Tarshish. I was not going to go BTL for these wicked Gentiles. Even if God told me to."

"I just want to add something here," John interjects. "The experience and decisions you made in Joppa were the same ones that faced Peter in the same city. Cornelius, the Roman centurion—like the Assyrians, an oppressor of Israel—was asked to do the following: 'Now send men to Joppa to bring back a man named Simon who is called Peter. He is staying with Simon the tanner, whose house is by the sea.'[52] The next afternoon at noon Peter went into a trance where he saw a sheet come down filled with unclean foods. He was asked to get up and eat them but refused. Ultimately out of this he learned a lesson that he shared once he arrived at the house of Cornelius. 'He said to them: "You are well aware that it is against our law for a Jew to associate with a Gentile or visit him. But God has shown me that I should not call any man impure or unclean."' I suppose, making your decision in Joppa, you still had to learn this."

"Absolutely! At this stage I wanted a fast boat *away* from the BTL challenge and the Gentiles. At first it looked like my plan to avoid this BTL act had worked. I went below decks and settled down to sleep. Avoiding BTL and hiding from God can be exhausting! My rest was short-lived. God had other plans. Before long we were trapped in a violent storm. I was forced to face the reality that God was not going to allow me to avoid this BTL act. I finally had to convince the sailors to throw me overboard, and immediately the storm subsided. We need to remember that our avoiding of BTL acts has implications not only for us but also for those around us.

"After I had been thrown overboard, God sent a huge fish to swallow me. I spent three days and three nights in the belly of the fish. Not pleasant, to say the least, but sometimes God needs to use whatever He can to get us back on course. It was dark, damp, and foul in the belly of

---

51   2 Kings 14:25.

52   Acts 10:5-6.

the fish. It was like a living death. I was afraid and had no idea if I would ever make it out alive. My plans were completely ruined. Ultimately we plan what we want to do, but God will set the BTL steps He requires us to take. We can't avoid them. Proverbs wisely says 'In his heart a man plans his course, but the Lord determines his steps.'[53]

"This time when God asked me to go to Nineveh, I did not argue. From the beach where the fish spat me out, it was a long way to Nineveh. I walked for many days and had time to reflect about what I was going to say. I thought I would keep it short and get to the point. I entered the city and boldly declared, 'Forty more days and Nineveh will be overturned.'[54] I really didn't want to deliver the message. I really didn't want to go BTL for these people. Then my worst fears were realized: they repented!"

"How did that make you feel" John asks

"I was angry and disappointed. I knew that our God is compassionate and that if they truly repented, He would not destroy them. To my amazement they repented, and God relented from destroying them. Things were turning out bad. They deserved to die. I felt let down and humiliated. I even prayed these words: 'Now, O Lord, take away my life, for it is better for me to die than to live.'[55] I know hearing me say it aloud sounds terrible. But how many of you have said or felt the same way when things don't go the way you expect them? How many of you have felt this angry when God forces you to go BTL when you just don't want to?

"The sad part is that the more I discussed this with God the more angry I got. In fact I asked God to take my life three times. I cannot begin to tell you how grateful I am that He is gracious, loving, and compassionate even toward someone like me.

"Then God asked me this question: 'Have you any right to be angry?'[56] Strangely though, He did not ask for my answer or give me any further response. In fact He chose a more powerful way of answering the question. He demonstrated it. God will also do the same in your life. When you doubt and resist the steps on your BTL spiritual growth,

---

[53]   Proverbs 16:9.

[54]   Jonah 3:4.

[55]   Jonah 4:3.

[56]   Jonah 4:4.

He will use circumstances around you to force you to reexamine your perspective."

"Jesus did it often," John adds. "He would use parables to get people to see how they were behaving and to draw personal lessons that profoundly changed their behavior."

Jonah acknowledges the point with a nod and then continues, "By now I felt that I had put a strong enough case forward for the destruction of the city. I wanted *my* will to be done. I made myself a shelter away from the city so that I could watch the destruction from a safe distance. Things seemed to once again be going my way. God caused a vine to grow up quickly that provided some shade and eased the stifling heat. I felt that finally things were coming right. God was obviously demonstrating His love and care for me. However, I had very little time to enjoy it. By dawn the next morning a hungry worm had chewed the vine so that it withered and died.

"We all have our worms in life—people or events that take away what we are enjoying. The lesson for us clear: do not look at who or what is eating away at your comfort but why. The why was the important point that God was about to demonstrate to me.

"By the time the sun was high in the sky, without my vine, I was very hot. Not only was it hot but also God sent a scorching wind from the east that made it worse. Here too is a lesson. God will sometimes make our adversity worse to make the realization and impact greater.

"I started to feel faint and just wanted to die. I was angry, hot, and tired. When God asked me if I had a right to be angry about the vine, my response was a definite and loud *yes*! Then came the aha moment, when the Lord said, 'You have been concerned about this vine, though you did not tend it or make it grow. It sprang up overnight and died overnight. But Nineveh has more than a hundred and twenty thousand people who cannot tell their right hand from their left, and many cattle as well. Should I not be concerned about that great city?'[57] I was letting my personal prejudices and views prevent me from going BTL for other people. I wanted unlimited grace and compassion for myself, while for others I wanted to limit this. I was being selfish and self-centered. In

---

[57] Jonah 4:10–11.

avoiding the call to go BTL and then wanting it to fail, I was failing the innocent, my God, and myself."

"We all go through aha moments when we see ourselves as God sees us," John responds. "Every one of these times we are shocked at what we see. Hopefully shocked enough to change our behavior.

"Jonah, thanks for sharing so candidly with us. I know that I have, at times, resisted some of the BTL acts God wanted me to perform, Ultimately He does know best, and because He loves us, He will not allow us to avoid them. Best we accept this and go BTL cheerfully and prayerfully."

With that John concludes the interview.

It's a Head Wind

You may have faced or be facing some strong head winds in your life at the moment. I would urge you to reflect on the why. Have you resisted the BTL step God wants you to take? Have you charted your own path?

Continuing with the nautical theme that pervades the story of Jonah, I would like to share a scripture that has been wonderfully and encouraging and inspiring for me. It comes from the Psalms.

> Others went out on the sea in ships;
>> they were merchants on the mighty waters.
> They saw the works of the Lord,
>> his wonderful deeds in the deep.
> For he spoke and stirred up a tempest
>> that lifted high the waves.
> They mounted up to the heavens and went down to the
>> depths;
>> in their peril their courage melted away.
> They reeled and staggered like drunken men;
>> they were at their wits' end.
> Then they cried out to the Lord in their trouble,
>> and he brought them out of their distress.
> He stilled the storm to a whisper;
>> the waves of the sea were hushed.
> They were glad when it grew calm,

and he guided them to their desired haven.
Let them give thanks to the Lord for his unfailing love
and his wonderful deeds for men.[58]

Does this sound familiar? When the BTL steps you are making fit with God's plan for you and are successful, you feel on a high. You acknowledge God in everything, and the love of Jesus shines out from you. Then you hit a head wind. You believe this is the correct path and the next BTL you should take. You decide to take things into our own hands. You get like Jonah and soon find yourself asking, what else could go wrong? Finally, you realize that God is in control. He is the only true guide. You then call on Him, and He hears. He saves you out of the distress you have created and brings you safely to the shelter of the port, because He loves and cares for you!

Jesus heeded the desperate pleas of His disciples in the midst of a furious storm on the lake. He rebuked the wind and waves, and it became completely calm. If you are looking for the haven of rest or calm in a tempestuous world, then why are you trying to go it alone? Follow the BTL steps set out for you, and call out if you need help.

It is that simple!

---

[58]   Psalm 107:23–31.

Chapter 10

Esther—Now Is Your Time

"Welcome, Esther—or should I call you by your Hebrew name, Hadassah?"

"Esther is fine," she politely responds.

"Esther, your story has captured the imagination of the world as an example of bravery and deliverance. In fact it is still celebrated today in the Jewish feast of Purim. You had one major BTL moment in your life that could have resulted in your death. Please talk us through the events leading up to this point and the BTL act itself."

"Sure, John," she responds with a quiet and peaceful tone. "I think it might useful to set some context to my life story. I was an orphan and one of the Jewish captives that Nebuchadnezzar had taken to Babylon. I lived in a time of oppression and sadness as the powerful and mighty King Xerxes of the Persian empire now ruled us. My upbringing was tough, but I was guided and kept by my cousin Mordecai who treated me as his own daughter. Our family, although now not recognized, had Jewish royal connections. My great grandfather was Kish, whose son, Saul, was the first King of Israel.

"My life then took an unexpected turn. King Xerxes divorced his wife Vashti due to her disobedience and asked that a search be made throughout the land to find a suitable replacement for her. I was taken to the palace and put under the care of the king's eunuch, Hegai. We were required to go through twelve months of beauty treatments and purification before we could see the king. It was stressful for all of us, as we were young. I was blessed to have the constant support of Mordecai. Every day he managed to get away from his palace duties for just enough time to check on me. Hegai also treated me very well, giving me seven maids and the best living quarters in the harem.

"God was truly directing my steps. He had a plan, and He was ensuring that it was going to work out for His glory. The only troubling thing was that I did not reveal my nationality, on Mordecai's instruction. I had agreed to do this because he had my best interests at heart and, since he worked in the palace, was aware of the internal politics. The formalities were very strictly adhered to. After the twelve months, the woman could select anything from the harem for her evening with the king. The next morning she would be placed under the care of another eunuch, Shaashgaz, who was in charge of the concubines. Only if the king summoned you by name would you return to him. There were no deviations from these rules, and it was made clear to us that nonadherence would result in death."

"It sounds like a very cold environment for a young girl," John points out sadly.

"It was. At a young age to be in such circumstances was very tough. I had lost my parents and now my cousin in the isolated environment of the palace. God puts us through these trying times as He prepares us for big BTL acts He wants us to take. At the time I could not have known the BTL act or role waiting for me, but I knew I needed to endure. When it became my turn to go to the king, I decided to get advice from Hegai about what to take with me."

"I remember reading of you that 'Esther won the favor of everyone who saw her.'[59] How did you achieve this?"

Esther gives a coy smile and replies, "It was not that I went looking for people to like me. I think the reason the Hegai and others supported me was that I always treated them with respect and humility. I knew in my heart that God was in control of these events and expected me to act in a manner pleasing to Him. The worst mistake we can make is to show arrogance at any time before or after BTL. It turns the message of what we are doing into self-praise, which is sure to result in unpleasant consequences."

---

[59] Esther 2:15.

"What is so encouraging is that similar words are said about our savior, Jesus," John comments. "It is recorded in Luke that 'Jesus grew in wisdom and stature, and in favor with God and men.'[60] I suppose this adds to what you were saying. If we are obedient and apply wisdom, we will naturally attract the favor of those around us—and, more important, the favor of God."

Esther nods in agreement and continues. "In the end the king was pleased with me, and I was made queen. As time went on, I continued to keep my nationality a secret and follow the instructions of Mordecai as I had done while he raised me. Too many young people believe that they are beyond advice and suffer the hard knocks of life relearning what they could have learned with open minds and hearts. I was glad to have the guidance of Mordecai, especially in an environment that was so foreign to me. We used to chat regularly, and it was during one of these meetings that he informed me about an assassination attempt being planned against King Xerxes. I told the king, and when it was investigated and found to be true, the would-be assassins were hanged, and I gave the credit to Mordecai. This small act of giving Mordecai the credit may have seemed insignificant at the time, but later it played a big part in God's deliverance of us as a nation. Sometimes people are tempted to take credit for other people's BTL acts. Mordecai had certainly gone BTL by informing me. I would like to caution all of your readers to be vigilant so as not to fall into this trap.

"Soon after this, things turned very nasty. King Xerxes decided to promote and honor a noble called Haman. Haman developed a hate for *all* Jews because Mordecai refused to bow to him as he passed through the palace gate. Haman managed to influence the king to send out messages throughout the land to kill all the Jews on a single day. The Jews were in despair and fear. Mordecai was dressed in sackcloth and weeping. He sent a message by my servant that I needed to go and see the king and plead for the deliverance of my people. I was afraid to do this. The king had not called me in thirty days, and going to see him without permission had one result: death!—unless he showed me mercy by holding out his golden scepter for me to touch. This was a big BTL act for me. One that could have cost me my life."

---

[60] Luke 2:52.

John leans forward. "So what made you make such a dangerous BTL step?"

"The powerful words of Mordecai. He said, If you remain silent at this time, relief and deliverance for the Jews will arise from another place, but you and your father's family will perish. And who knows but that you have come to royal position for such a time as this?'[61] God had set me in position for this very moment. I needed to act. My time was now. The line was scary, but to turn away from it would have meant death for my people and me. The people needed a savior, and I was their only hope at this time. I had to go BTL. So I did, but not right away. I asked Mordecai to gather all the Jews in the city and fast and pray for me for three days. After this I was going to see the king, and if I died, then that was part of the plan of God. The three days was not only to get support in prayer but also for me to prepare myself. I can highly recommend that any of you facing life-changing BTL acts should allow time to meditate and commune with God. It is an important part of preparing for the pressure and chaos of the act itself.

"As it turned out, God allowed the situation to unfold in such a way that Haman was hanged on the gallows he had prepared for Mordecai. Mordecai was honored, and the Jews were saved from annihilation. I was left asking myself the ultimate question. What if I had not gone BTL?"

"That is the question we all need to ask ourselves," John adds gravely. "I have found our discussion very informative and challenging. When I look at what you had to endure, I am ashamed of all the times I have shrunk back or stepped back from the line. God will get someone to go BTL. Let's all develop the obedience, wisdom, and faith to go BTL when we are called. Who knows, maybe God will be using you to save a man, woman, child, or even a nation."

The 3 Ts

When I read about Esther, I am drawn to the words that Proverbs uses to describe the wife and women of noble character. It says, "Charm is deceptive, and beauty is fleeting; but a woman who fears the Lord is

---

[61]   Esther 4:14.

to be praised."[62] Esther had everything that you would admire from an outward appearance. However, what was important was that she put God first. Earlier in Proverbs 31 it describes this woman as showing "strength and dignity" as well as "wisdom."[63] What a fine example Esther is of this. She clearly understood and practiced the 3 Ts. We all need a daily dose of the 3 T vitamins!

First you have to *Trust*. Trust that God is in control and that he is guiding your steps even when the BTL challenge seems so difficult and dangerous that you want to run as far from it as possible.

Second is *Tolerance*. Tolerance speaks of the biblical principle of patiently waiting. There is a difference between waiting and waiting patiently! You may find that at some junctures of your life you can very easily wait patiently. I have found that this is easy when things are good. When things get tough or a huge BTL challenge looms, I am less inclined to wait for the Lord's support in His time.

Third is *Tenacity*. This is the ability to keep going when others give up. It is a key part of your spiritual growth. As you see the big BTL act getting closer and closer, the inclination is to give up. Fear has a way of undermining what you knew was true when you started your spiritual journey.

There are many stories of people who through the ages have gone BTL. In some cases it has cost them their lives. The very Bible that we have before us in English has cost many people their lives. I am always moved to read of these men and women who through the ages risked everything to ensure that the masses could get access to the Bible in their own language. For example, in 1415 John Hus was stripped, secured to a stake, and burnt to death. His sacrifice, along with those before and after, him means a great deal in the lives of millions today.

Many of us are not called to go BTL in such a dramatic fashion. You are, however, expected to be fully committed to our Father. Moses' last words clearly demonstrate the choices you make every time you stand *before* the line.

---

[62]   Proverbs 31:30.

[63]   Proverbs 31:25–26.

This day I call heaven and earth as witnesses against you that I have set before you life and death, blessings and curses. Now choose life, so that you and your children may live and that you may love the Lord your God, listen to his voice, and hold fast to him. For the Lord is your life, and he will give you many years in the land he swore to give to your fathers, Abraham, Isaac and Jacob.[64]

Did you notice the 3 Ts? Loving God means you trust Him. Listening to Him allows you to tolerate any situation, knowing He is in control. Holding fast means never giving up or Tenacity.

Like Moses I urge you to choose life in Jesus and keep faithful to the path of life!

---

[64] Deuteronomy 30:19-20.

Chapter 11

Ruth—All for Love

"You are a woman with a big heart. Your name has four letters, just like the love you show to all around you. Ruth, thanks for making yourself available for this first edition of BTL."

"Hi, John," she responds in a soft and soothing voice. "It's lovely to be here with you."

"I saw you and Esther talking at the lift and was wondering what you were chatting about."

Ruth gives a broad smile. "We were just chatting about how God has worked in both our lives and how we were both unaware of how the small BTL decisions in our lives would have huge implications for the future."

"That brings me conveniently to our subject for this discussion: going BTL in our lives." John fixes her with a searching look and asks, "How did going BTL influence the direction and outcome of your life, and what was that outcome?"

"Well, my life story begins with *lots* of tragedy. I still believe that God works best with us when we feel our lowest and lost—if we will allow Him to. In my native Moab, I had met and married a man called Mahlon from Bethlehem in Judah. His mother and father had moved from Judah to escape the severe famine in the land. One of the first things that struck me about the family was the pivotal role that their mother, Naomi, played in her two sons' lives. This role was severely challenged when her husband died; then, ten years after I married Mahlon, he and his brother both died. It was a trying time for all of us, but most especially for Naomi. She was in a foreign country with her two daughters-in-law. It was then that we got news that things had improved in Judah, and

Naomi decided that she should go back to her own people and land. We, of course, accompanied her on the way back to Judah."

"Why do you say 'of course'?" John asks, looking a little confused. "You were not required by any law to go with her."

Ruth again smiles and continues. "It seemed the obvious thing to do as she had been a massive influence in both my and Orpah's lives over the ten years we had been married to her sons. That was why we wept so bitterly when she asked us to go back to our people and find new husbands. It was so typical of the type of person Naomi was. Determined, kind, loving, and practical all rolled into one! She called us her daughters and treated us that way. She urged us to go back to Moab in part because she felt that God was against her and that there was no need for us to share in her pain.

"Then came the moment. The line had been drawn and I could either cross it or walk away without any fear of offence. Orpah decided to leave and go back to Moab. She was very sad to say good-bye but decided that it was the most logical decision, and Naomi's advice made sense. I agreed that it made sense but refused to let go of Naomi. I clung to her. My mind was made up, and I was going BTL to a future I didn't understand, to a people I didn't know, but with a person I loved and cared for deeply. Naomi was my rock in such uncertain times."

John's face lights up as he makes a connection that he then shares. "What you have said about clinging to Naomi reminds me of a passage in Romans. It says 'Love must be sincere. Hate what is evil; cling to what is good.'[65] Your sincere love and commitment directed your BTL act. I suppose in this lies the lesson. If we are sincere and genuine in our love for someone or something, then we will be motivated enough to go BTL. It makes it easier to differentiate what has to be done and what has to be avoided."

Ruth interrupts John with a light touch on the arm. "And more than that is the power of the example we set for those around us. If Naomi had not set the example she did, would I have followed? If Naomi had not loved the Lord, would I have? Fathers, mothers, leaders, and friends have to consider the example they are setting for those around them.

---

[65]   Romans 12:9.

Are they encouraging or discouraging them about their opportunity to go BTL?

"The example I had made it easy to go BTL for love. She still tried to convince me to stay because she was concerned about my needs. It was then I had to do what many of you may get called to do, that is to confirm emphatically that you will not be persuaded. It is worth thinking though what you will face before you go BTL. I had, so I could easily say these words:'Don't urge me to leave you or to turn back from you. Where you go I will go, and where you stay I will stay. Your people will be my people and your God my God. Where you die I will die, and there I will be buried. May the Lord deal with me, be it ever so severely, if anything but death separates you and me.'[66] After I said this, Naomi stopped trying to convince me to go back; I had confirmed to her that I realized how much my life would change BTL. I would need to live where she chose to live. I had to accept being part of a different people, and I had to follow her God. Sometimes we go BTL and try to change circumstances to suit us. If we go BTL in love then, we should allow ourselves to be changed."

John nods. "Too often people want to change things to be more comfortable for them. It's tough to accept new things but, as you say, if we go with the correct attitude BTL, then we are more likely to succeed."

"I needed to keep this attitude in mind when we arrived in Bethlehem. We caused a stir when we arrived, especially since I was from Moab. Keep in mind that this all occurred at the time of the Judges, and not long before this my country had under King Eglon invaded the land and made the people subject to us for eighteen years. They were eventually delivered by the actions of Ehud, but the memories of those times remained. I could feel the eyes trained on me but chose to ignore them.

"Naomi and I needed grain, and as it was time for the barley harvest, I decided to go work in the fields. God guided me into the field of a relative of Naomi's husband by the name of Boaz. My plan was to go behind the harvesters and pick up any grain that was left behind. I worked hard, even through the heat of the day. As with any BTL act,

---

[66]   Ruth 1:16-17.

we still need to work *beyond* the line. I realized this, and it drew me to Boaz's attention. He arranged that his harvesters were not to bother me and offered me access to water from his well. His kindness to me, a foreigner from Moab, surprised me. His response was very revealing. 'I've been told all about what you have done for your mother-in-law since the death of your husband—how you left your father and mother and your homeland and came to live with a people you did not know before. May the Lord repay you for what you have done. May you be richly rewarded by the Lord, the God of Israel, under whose wings you have come to take refuge.'[67] The private BTL act I had done out of love had been made public. He knew that I had committed to follow Naomi and, more important, that I trusted the only true God to protect me.

"We must never ever underestimate the loving care of our Father. In this strange place with these strange circumstances He was working behind the scenes to help me. I was truly blessed during both the barley and wheat harvest and remained to work in the fields of Boaz. Then Naomi decided in her love and care that I could not remain alone. She orchestrated events and guided me to ensure that eventually Boaz and I got married. I am still amazed that when we show love, it comes back many times more. My love for Naomi came back in so many more ways—from her, from Boaz, and from God. What a wonderful thing it is to love and be loved!

"The greatest part of this love of God was revealed by the fact that God allowed me to have a child. When I was with Mahlon and living in Moab, I could not have children. At the time it greatly concerned me. God, however, had other plans. He could see a path or ladder I needed to climb. I needed to take a bold BTL step, and then things would change. We had a son and called him Obed; he was the grandfather of King David. God always blesses us BTL in ways that we can't even begin to imagine."

John decides to take this opportunity to close off the interview. "Ruth, thanks for reminding us of the power of love. You truly are a reflection of love, and your story demonstrates how going BTL for love can have such wonderful rewards in our lives."

---

[67]   Ruth 2:11-12.

The Lesson of Love

Love is an emotive word with powerful associations. You need to use it, or it will fade and die. When you truly love, then going BTL is made much easier. The chapter of love in the Bible is 1 Corinthians 13. It defines for you the kinds of characteristics that are revealed by sincere and true love. "Love is patient, love is kind. It does not envy, it does not boast, it is not proud. It is not rude, it is not self-seeking, it is not easily angered, it keeps no record of wrongs. Love does not delight in evil but rejoices with the truth. It always protects, always trusts, always hopes, always perseveres."[68] What an exhaustive list! What is frightening is to ask yourself how many of these characteristics you show. I know that I battle more with some of these than with others, but I also know that if I want to receive love, I must give love. The more your love grows, the easier it is to go BTL.

If you are still not motivated enough then consider these words from Jesus. "Greater love has no one than this, that he lay down his life for his friends."[69] Jesus considers you to be His friend and gave His life for you. He expects you to behave in the same way to those around you. This means you need to demonstrate love.

I have been greatly encouraged by the work of many Christian outreach programs around the world. The principle that Jesus demonstrated, of touch then teach, is gaining momentum every day. I have had the privilege of being a part of some of these initiatives. One involved building preschools and community centers for underprivileged communities in South Africa. These cute little children, all between the ages of 3 three and seven, are so wonderful to behold. They brim over with love, even though they have nothing—and I mean nothing. Often they don't get food at home, and some of them suffer from the scourge of HIV. Yet even with all this they find peace, love, and security at these schools where they are fed, taught and loved. They touch your heart with the sincerity and purity of their love.

So can you use Ruth "speak"?

---

[68]　1 Corinthians 13:4-7.

[69]　John 15:13.

Don't urge me to leave you or to turn back from you. Where you go I will go, and where you stay I will stay. Your people will be my people and your God my God. Where you die I will die, and there I will be buried. May the Lord deal with me, be it ever so severely, if anything but death separates you and me.[70]

Whom have you touched or inspired with your love to go BTL? Has the love of Jesus moved you to act and go BTL for Him?

---

[70]   Ruth 1:16–17.

Chapter 12

Peter—Failure and Love

"You have been called the Rock. I call you a friend and fellow disciple. Peter, a very warm welcome to BTL!"

"Hi, John!" Peter responds excitedly.

"It is so nice for me to interview you," John comments. "We have shared many special moments together, and I look forward to discussing some of your BTL acts. Knowing how passionate you are about teaching others to go BTL, I have selected only a few moments in your life that I felt would help our audience the most."

"No problem, I am in your very capable hands," Peter answers. He radiates confidence, and his voice is powerful and strong.

John smiles and continues. "Well, I hope you are still as trusting once the interview is over. So let's kick off with the first BTL act I want to focus on. I felt that this particular story is worth looking at in detail. I would like you to talk us though the night that you decided to walk on water. What made you do it?"

"I suppose the short answer is Why not?" Peter responds with a grin. "I have always been someone who acted and reacted on what I feel passionate about. With this in mind, let me share the events of that night.

"Jesus had just performed the miracle of feeding more than five thousand people and now asked us to go ahead of Him to the other side of the lake. There was nothing extraordinary about the request; the Master often liked to spend time alone in meditation and prayer. So we left that evening and set off. When we were some distance from the shore, a violent storm came up, and we were in real danger. We were alone, frightened, and without Jesus.

"We tried everything we knew to withstand the forces of the weather. Some of us were experienced fisherman and knew how to handle the boat. But by sometime after midnight we were exhausted, tired, and fearing death. The wind was howling, and waves were crashing over the boat. Nothing we tried was working, and we were not making headway toward shelter.

"In our darkest hour, Jesus came to us. When we first saw Him we were afraid not knowing what to make of this, which only intensified our fear. Then through the sounds of the wind and waves we heard His voice. 'Take courage! It is I. Don't be afraid.'[71] Often when all seems lost, if we listen and look, we will see Jesus. He is never far away. We all rejoiced to see Him, and my heart leaped for joy. I just wanted to be with Him and asked if I could go to Him on the water. He responded with one word—the same word He uses to invite all people to Him today: 'Come.'[72] I wanted to be with Jesus. I had received the invite and was ready to go BTL. I didn't leap overboard but rather gingerly climbed out of the boat and started walking on the water toward Jesus. I had done it and was on my way to Jesus.

"Then I saw the wind and waves and forgot about the man in front of me. Like many of us I had gone BTL with confidence, but when I saw the challenges BTL, I was afraid and started sinking. I realized that I needed help, and only one person could give it. I was not going to swim my way out of this or rely on my friends to pull me out. I needed real help and shouted at the top of my voice, 'Lord, save me!' So many people, when struggling BTL, forget there is help close at hand. Jesus reached out at once and caught me. 'You of little faith,' He said, 'why did you doubt?'[73] He did not delay. I called, and He responded. This is very comforting in difficult times BTL. I suppose the key lesson out of this is that I needed to trust BTL. I needed to keep focused on Jesus rather than the negative things around me.

"It's a lesson we all need to remember when we encounter such worrying and trying times," John adds. "We all know of the many courageous and difficult BTL moments in your life. I would like to talk,

---

[71]   Matthew 14:27.

[72]   Matthew 14:29.

[73]   Matthew 14:30–31.

though, about when you failed to go BTL, as this also has instructive value for us. I wonder if you could talk us through the night that you denied Jesus."

Peter winces at the mention of the word deny but bravely chooses to share his thoughts. "It was a night full of emotion. The events prior to this had seen many ups and downs for me personally. During the Passover supper Jesus spoke of how He would be betrayed. I felt that this could not be and said, 'Lord, I am ready to go with you to prison and to death.'[74] My passion was honest and true, but Jesus knew the challenges that lay before me in order to perform this BTL act. I was warned. Jesus warned me that I would that very night deny Him three times before the cock should crow. Unfortunately I chose to ignore the warning."

"You are not alone in that," John comments gravely. "Most of us have had times when we ignored warnings. I know in my own life I have ignored similar warnings that, if heeded, would have allowed me to go BTL. The issue is how to deal with the failure to go BTL when you have been warned. How did you react?"

"It was extremely tough," Peter replies sadly. "It did feel worse because I knew better. I looked at the line and hung back. Not once but three times. I denied Him three times. Then the hardest moment of all. The Lord turned and looked straight at me. Then I remembered the word the Lord had spoken to me: 'Before the rooster crows today, you will disown me three times.'[75] That look—I will never forget it. It was sadness. He had tried to warn me that this line was approaching, but I was so busy shouting about my loyalty, I failed to prepare.

"I urge your readers to please be vigilant in their spiritual walk. Listen for the warnings, and prepare to overcome when the line is presented. Step boldly BTL, so that you never have to see that look from Jesus."

John sees that Peter is struggling with his emotions at this point and decides to step in. "Peter, I do remember these words that Jesus said to you at our Passover meal: 'I have prayed for you, Simon, that your faith may not fail. And when you have turned back, strengthen your brothers.'[76] What did He mean by this?"

---

[74] Luke 22:33.

[75] Luke 22:34, 60–62.

[76] Luke 22:32.

Peter looks relieved to be moving on and quickly responds. "Well, there were several clues in this. First, my faith was going to be tried, and I would fail to go BTL on this occasion. I must not let this one mistake keep me from continuing on the path laid out for me. Second, once I had come to peace with my failure, I needed to use what I have learned to strengthen those around me that there is hope and forgiveness for lines we have not crossed. The reality of this was brought home to me once our Master was raised from the dead.

"It happened when we went fishing and caught an abundance of fish after He told us to throw the net on the other side. I remember that you were the first to recognize that it was the Lord." says Peter, looking at John.

"The minute you identified it was Him, I was not going to wait. This time I did not try and walk on water. I jumped in and swam the hundred yards to the shore where He had some burning coals, fish on the fire, and some bread. When we finished eating, He asked me three times if I loved Him. I told Him that I loved Him, and He asked me to feed and take care of His sheep. I got the message loud and clear. Yes, I had doubted and sunk below the water on the stormy lake. This time I leaped in and swam with purpose to be with Him. Yes, I had denied Him three times, but He had confirmed three times that I loved Him. My BTL failure allowed me to empathize with those around me who also failed at times. It made me more real and a better leader to spread the gospel.

"Please don't mistake me. I am not advocating that we fail to go BTL for Jesus. What I am saying is that there is hope beyond our failures. We are forgiven when we turn around or repent. The next line will come, the way it did for me. All we need to do is be ready this time to go BTL."

"Peter, I think this would be the ideal place for us to end our interview," John says. "I know that we all have learned from what you had to say tonight. We need to learn to rise from the ashes of our failures and pursue the next line, in the hope that this time we will go BTL."

Warning Lights and Fear

Fear can be crippling for your faith. In previous chapters I showed how it can prevent us from going BTL. You need to develop the heart and mind of Peter. The Casting Crowns so beautifully put it in these words from their song "Voice of Truth":

> Oh what I would do to have
> The kind of faith it takes to climb out of the boat I'm in
> Onto the crashing waves
>
> To step out of my comfort zone
> To the realm of the unknown where Jesus is
> And He's holding out His hand

Going BTL is an act of faith. You are moving out of your comfort zone. You need to be bold and not doubt. You need to focus your attention on Jesus

I have flown helicopters for many years now. I find the experience of flying above the earth invigorating and love to share it with as many people as possible. One of the key things you are taught when learning to fly is the ability to recognize and respond to warning lights. The first step is to see and understand what the warning light is. There is a panel of lights with some in red and some in orange, based on the severity of the emergency. As in your life, you need to look for these warning signs. God warns you through His words in the Bible and by working in your life to reveal the path you should take.

The next step is to respond to the warning lights. One of the areas that the aviation industry still grapples with is how to accurately predict how a pilot will react in a real crisis situation. Some people freeze while others remain calm. Losing your cool in an aircraft will get you killed. Losing your cool BTL will result in failure.

Finally we are taught how to respond. We practice and practice emergencies like engine failure, tail-rotor failure, etc. The reason we practice is so that, when we are called to act, it becomes almost second nature. In your life you will encounter difficulties and failures. The point is to keep learning from them so that next time they occur you know how to respond.

We have all failed sometime or another. Don't let your BTL failures destroy your love for Jesus. See the warnings, respond, and keep learning. Most important of all, keep going BTL!

Chapter 13

Stephen — Lies and Vision

J ohn begins. "You have been called a man of grace, power, and wisdom. You gave your life for the gospel. Welcome, Stephen."

"Thanks, John," Stephen responds in a measured and prominent voice. "I look forward to sharing with you."

"To start with, could you talk us through how you got to the point of your trial and your ultimate BTL act?"

Stephen straightens in his seat almost as if preparing for some formal presentation. "I was chosen by the twelve apostles to be part of a group of seven Grecian Jews tasked with ensuring that our widows were not overlooked when it came to the daily distribution of food. The selection criteria were simple. They were looking for men full of the Spirit and wisdom. Here is the first clue to going BTL for the big, scary, and challenging acts: Keep close to God, and apply wisdom to all your decisions."

"What I find interesting," John interjects, "are these words said of you at that time: 'This proposal pleased the whole group. They chose Stephen, a man full of faith and of the Holy Spirit; also Philip, Procorus, Nicanor, Timon, Parmenas, and Nicolas from Antioch, a convert to Judaism.'[77] You were specifically identified as someone full of faith and the Holy Spirit."

"Yes, but as you know the Scripture tells us that more is expected from those with more talents," Stephen responds immediately. "It was a time of great wonder and miracles. I was on a spiritual high as I went around healing and teaching in the name of Jesus. My faith was secure

---

[77]   Acts 6:5.

and strong, and the power of God was prevalent in my life. I could feel and see that God was working with me. Jews in the regions where I preached started to resent the works that God was doing through me and were constantly debating the calling of the gospel."

Once again John interjects. "Is it true they found it impossible to defeat you in these debates?"

Stephen laughs and then responds, "It was not a competition as far as I was concerned. They just could not find any reason besides their own prejudices and pride to withstand the wisdom of Scripture and the example of Jesus. Here is a second clue for our learning. Expect that when you clearly show others the only true and life-giving way, sometimes the shaking of deep-seated beliefs can unhinge the most logical of minds. When this happens, you will find desperate and angry people willing to do anything to reclaim their mistaken beliefs. These are dangerous people, as I was soon to discover."

"You are described as 'a man full of God's grace and power.'[78] Did you need to draw on this as the BTL challenge drew closer?" John asks.

"Absolutely! We all need to remember that power without grace is wasted. Simply demonstrating God's power without grace would not have been a true reflection of the life and love of Jesus. This delicate balance is essential to a healthy Christian life and one that I tried to maintain even in the darkest hours that were fast approaching."

"How does it feel to be accused, like Jesus, of something you didn't do?" John asks with a sense of dread.

"As one would expect, it is very upsetting and frustrating, but you need to deal with it. My BTL act was born out of a lie. Sometimes we are challenged to go BTL in defense of truth. I knew this was a setup, but I was not going to stoop to retaliate with personal attacks. Instead I decide that I had been presented with the ideal opportunity to state the case of the gospel. They had accused me of blasphemy against Moses and God. For good measure they felt it necessary to add the same accusation they made against our Lord, that He would destroy the temple. Interesting that this time they didn't add the bit that after three days a temple without hands would be raised!

---

[78] Acts 6:8.

"All these accusations were made against me before the Council, and while they were accusing me, I was already focusing BTL. I had a clear vision. I knew where I needed to go. I was so close to my God in mind and in Spirit that I had already gone BTL in my mind."

John responds, "That must be why Scripture says that 'the Sanhedrin looked intently at Stephen, and they saw that his face was like the face of an angel.'"[79]

"I suppose," Stephen responds hesitantly. "I could not see my own face but assume that, because I was approaching such a significant BTL act, in my focus I had drawn close to God in a way similar to Moses. 'When Moses came down from Mount Sinai with the two tablets of the Testimony in his hands, he was not aware that his face was radiant because he had spoken with the Lord.'[80] Always remember that God is near when we need Him. Just make the effort to draw close and speak to Him.

"The Sanhedrin was now ready to accuse me and wanted me to defend myself against all the specific charges. I decided to take a different approach. I took them through our own history, showing how God worked through the lives of Abraham, Joseph, Moses, David, and Solomon. These men of faith and these major BTLs bore testimony to the work of the Holy Spirit. I accused my listeners of having uncircumcised hearts and ears like those of their fathers. They were accusing me of wanting to change the Law of Moses. I also knew they were very familiar with the Law, so I used the Law to accuse them. My words would have reminded them of these words in the Law: 'if they will confess *their sins and the sins of their fathers*—their treachery against me and their hostility toward me, which made me hostile toward them so that I sent them into the land of their enemies—then when their *uncircumcised hearts* are humbled and they pay for their sin, I will remember my covenant with Jacob and my covenant with Isaac and my covenant with Abraham, and I will remember the land.'[81] They just couldn't see it. They needed humility and not pride. They needed to acknowledge and not deny. They needed love and not hostility. Here is a massive lesson for all of us not to resist

---

[79] Acts 6:15.

[80] Exodus 34:29.

[81] Leviticus 26:40–42.

others who are going BTL. We need to examine our true motives in defending what we believe to be the correct path. Are you sure you're correct?"

Stephen then continues. He now seems even more focused and intense. "They didn't want to hear this. Their anger boiled over and they were ready to kill. I however saw another scene. I saw Jesus, and He was standing at the right hand of God. I saw the glory of God and basked in its warmth. My vision was real and exciting, so I called out to the Sanhedrin. I said, 'Look, I see heaven open and the Son of Man standing at the right hand of God.'[82] This was of course the final straw. They grabbed me and dragged me outside the city. They took large stones and started stoning me to death. As I fell bloodied and bashed to my knees, I could still see Jesus. As each stone crashed into my body, I could still see Jesus. As the blood dripped into my eyes, I could still see Jesus. And He touched my heart. I asked Him not to make them pay for their sins. After all, He was the true example of love and forgiveness."

"This story has a further twist in that when they stoned you they left their clothes at the feet of a then-young man called Saul, who later became the apostle Paul.´

"Yes, that is true. I suppose that is the final clue in my BTL act. Even though my defense had meant nothing to all those blinded hard hearts and minds, Jesus had a plan. A plan to turn a man's life upside down and force him to look at the things I said in a fresh way."

John wraps up the interview: "Thank you, Stephen, for sharing such a powerful BTL act."

No Vision = No Hope

Without vision you will feel lost. It gives you direction beyond your current circumstances and gives you an anchor to which to secure yourself. Vision should also be the wellspring of your positive thinking and attitude. Actually, it should go further than this. People should see your joy and hope shining on your face. As Proverbs says, "As water reflects a face, so a man's heart reflects the man."[83] Like Stephen you

---

[82] Acts 7:56.

[83] Proverbs 27:19.

should outwardly display the fact that you do see Jesus, that even in your toughest BTL challenge you can see BTL.

I have found it useful to frequently revisit my vision. It includes spiritual, family, and financial goals. Being a visual person, I have put pictures of what I want to achieve on a slide. It makes it very easy to scan a single page and realign my goals. To me the vision is so real that I can see it as already accomplished. I know that God will guide me as I strive to achieve the goals and that, as I travel my path, I will make slight adjustments based on His guidance. Ultimately, I focus on ensuring that everything I strive for allows me to serve Him better, as that is what He calls me to do.

I come from a family with vision. Both my father and my two brothers started businesses from the garage. When I was a child, my father left a job at a secure major company to go it alone. He started from our home with no customers and a workshop that used to be our garage. My brothers completed successful university studies and started an IT company from the garage. All of them were successful, which has allowed them to share and give more to their family, the church, and those in need. They would never have been able to take these bold moves if they did not have vision. Did they have tough months and years? Of course! What helped them overcome was the vision of what lay ahead.

So what lies ahead of you? Can you see it? Really see it?

Get the vision, and keep it as you go BTL!

Chapter 14

Paul—A New View

"Paul, thanks for joining me today," John begins enthusiastically. "Your BTL acts are many and varied in nature, but I want to start with the one that changed your life forever. Please, could you talk us through what happened to you on the way to Damascus from Jerusalem?"

"With pleasure, John," Paul responds in a deliberate, strong tone. "My life was at that stage on a clear course. I was climbing the Jewish religious ladder. I had devout parents who had sent me to be taught by one of the most respected Jewish teachers, called Gamaliel. I was zealous for the ways of the Law and God. I was unmoved by the stoning of Stephen and was rounding up and imprisoning Christians as often as I could. My path was set, and the direction was clear. With this in mind, I asked for letters from the high priest authorizing me to go to Damascus and arrest those who followed the Christian way in that city.

"As I neared Damascus, my life changed forever. Jesus knew that I would not go BTL and change my life completely unless something major happened. I needed an intervention!"

John laughs and adds, "Paul, I think we all need a intervention sometimes. We get so focused and dogmatic about what we believe is true that we lose sight of what could be."

"Absolutely!" Paul responds emphatically. "There is no way that I would have changed my way if Jesus had not stopped me on that road."

"Your story reminds me so much of Balaam, son of Beor. Balak, the king of Moab, asked him to come and curse Israel. After little persuasion, he took to the road with the purpose of causing harm to God's people. His intervention came from an angel, brandishing a drawn sword, standing ready to kill him. He could not see the angel, but his donkey could—the same donkey he was beating furiously as it deviated from the path three times. 'Then the Lord opened Balaam's eyes, and he saw the angel of the Lord standing in the road with his sword drawn. So he bowed low and fell facedown.

"'The angel of the Lord asked him, "Why have you beaten your donkey these three times? I have come here to oppose you because your path is a reckless one before me. The donkey saw me and turned away from me these three times. If she had not turned away, I would certainly have killed you by now, but I would have spared her."'[84] Would you agree that, like Balaam's, your path was reckless?" John asks.

"Yes, I had also justified my actions in my mind and heart. Only after the intervention caused me to go BTL did I fully understand how reckless I was being. My U-turn was at whiplash speeds, with bright lights from heaven, Jesus talking to me, and then blindness for three days. The blindness was the key as I now no longer was in charge. I had to rely on other people to lead me by the hand to Damascus, and then I had to trust that I would be healed. I went to stay with Judas who lived in Straight Street in Damascus and waited."

"That must have been a tense time," John comments. "Scripture tells us that while you were waiting, the Lord was speaking to a disciple named Ananias to go and heal you. He of course was reluctant to help the man who was persecuting the Christians. He too needed to go through a bit of a mind shift—an intervention of sorts. He was then told in no uncertain terms to go."

Paul smiles as he recalls the event. "Yes, he arrived at Judas's house sounding apprehensive and a little scared. He had obviously rehearsed what he was going to say." Paul chuckles. "His words were for my benefit as much as his. He said, 'Brother Saul, the Lord—Jesus, who appeared to you on the road as you were coming here—has sent me so that you may see again and be filled with the Holy Spirit.'[85] You see how he was emphasizing that now we were brothers, that it was Jesus who sent him, and that he had a gift to give. Sight and the Holy Spirit! I don't blame him for feeling confused and scared. We both were performing BTL acts in somewhat uncharted waters. Not only did I get my sight back; I got a

---

[84] Numbers 22:31–33.
[85] Acts 9:17.

new vision, a vision that included serving Jesus. Godly interventions are given to force us to reevaluate and step BTL in a new direction. They are shocking and hard but necessary if we are to follow the correct path. They are another example of the love that Jesus has for us."

John interjects and says, "I would just like to pick up on your point of not only having your physical eyesight but a new outlook on life and now doing God's will. Once again, I believe Balaam went though the same learning process. When he realized that it pleased God to bless Israel, then he also showed how his vision had changed as a result of the intervention. 'The oracle of Balaam son of Beor, the oracle of one whose eye sees clearly, the oracle of one who hears the words of God, who sees a vision from the Almighty, who falls prostrate, and whose eyes are opened.'"[86]

"Yes, an intervention to go BTL in a completely new direction has a profound effect on your vision. It is absolutely critical to have this in cases such as Balaam and mine when you are going to be faced with lots of skeptics and opposition. The good news is that I personally can attest that, when I started to preach and prove that Jesus was the only way, I seemed to grow and grow in confidence and strength.

"I had my challenges. The Jews were trying to kill me, and the disciples in Jerusalem were hiding from me. Not the ideal start to my new direction. You will also find similar challenges and temptations once you have gone through an intervention BTL act. Thrive and survive by keeping your eyes wide open to the new vision before you."

"You faced a lot of tough physical challenges in your walk," John notes. "Would you say that, by going BTL, you really did put your life at risk?"

"I had my fair share," Paul replies. "After I arrived in Jerusalem, back from Damascus, the Grecian Jews tried to kill me, and I had to leave again. This happened a lot. Sometimes I did get away, but sometimes not. 'Five times I received from the Jews the forty lashes minus one. Three times I was beaten with rods, once I was stoned, three times I was shipwrecked, I spent a night and a day in the open sea, I have been constantly on the move. I have been in danger from rivers, in danger from bandits, in danger from my own countrymen, in danger from Gentiles; in danger

---

[86] Numbers 24:3-4.

in the city, in danger in the country, in danger at sea; and in danger from false brothers. I have labored and toiled and have often gone without sleep; I have known hunger and thirst and have often gone without food; I have been cold and naked.'[87] I mention this for two reasons. First, you will not find it easy once you take up your new path. Second, these hardships are part of our learning. In my case the things I faced highlighted my weakness and need for Jesus in my life."

"You mention that you were stoned once. Tell us about this."

Paul seems to flinch at the mention of stoning. "As you are aware, I was present and consented to the stoning of Stephen. Through my stoning I came to realize the power of what he taught that day and the pain he experienced.

"Barnabas and I were in Lystra and healed a man lame from birth. The local people thought we were the gods in human form and wanted to bow down and sacrifice to us. We had to urgently interrupt and explain that they should not worship us but Jesus. Seizing the opportunity to win over the crowd, some Jews who had followed us from Pisidian Antioch and Iconium convinced the crowd to turn on me. They then stoned me. I felt all the pain of the stones hitting me and could clearly recall Stephen suffering the same way. I could also see BTL. My eyes were open to the mission to which Jesus was calling me. They dragged my bloodied and bruised body outside the city, thinking I was dead. The disciples also believed I was dead and gathered around me to pray. As they arrived, I got up, much to their shock and horror, and went back into the city."

"Is it true that the next day you left for Derbe to continue preaching the gospel?" John asks.

"Yes," Paul replies, "and we went back to Lystra after that. There is work to be done BTL, and we need to keep going."

"Well, Paul you have given us much food for thought. We may face intervention BTL moments in our lives and need to remember that, no matter how tough or frightening it may seem, we need to keep working for Jesus."

---

[87] 2 Corinthians 11:24–27.

Your Addiction

Addictions have a way of clouding how you act and behave. No matter what others may say, you cannot see it. In many cases the only way to get you to break out of the wrong way is an intervention. Anyone who has gone through one will tell you that they are tough, frightening, and challenging. Its purpose is to get you, like Paul, to break out of a destructive pattern. It does, however, require you to go BTL. You need to act. You need to agree to go in the new direction and get the treatment you need. You need to understand that it will be hard and long. You also need the vision of what lies beyond all the pain of the BTL act itself. Finally, you need to accept that you are always still prone to making the same mistakes and going back to the old path. You are always a recovering addict!

You will recall that we were addicted to the wrong things before we followed Jesus. We still have a propensity to sin. We are all recovering sinners! It is good to remember this as you follow the path laid out for you. Don't flirt with danger; ensure that you gain strength in prayer and from fellow Christians. Paul says, "Let us consider how we may spur one another on toward love and good deeds. Let us not give up meeting together, as some are in the habit of doing, but let us encourage one another—and all the more as you see the Day approaching."[88] If you want to know about a *bad* habit, then there it is! In two verses Paul uses the words *encourage* and *spur on*. He is directing us to support each in the tough times.

Why do you think organizations such as Alcoholics Anonymous have regular meetings? They do it so that they can share their weekly trials and support each other. They go further than this and appoint a sponsor to be available to give personal advice, support and guidance twenty-four hours a day. You have someone like this, and His name is Jesus! He has intervened in your life and wants to help you. He is available twenty-four hours a day. He does not judge you. He loves you and wants you to overcome your sinful addictions.

Peter has some strong warnings for us. He warns us to be careful not to go back to our old ways when we are enticed by false teachers:

---

[88] Hebrews 10:24-25.

They have left the straight way and wandered off to follow the way of Balaam son of Beor, who loved the wages of wickedness. But he was rebuked for his wrongdoing by a donkey—a beast without speech—who spoke with a man's voice and restrained the prophet's madness.

These men are springs without water and mists driven by a storm. Blackest darkness is reserved for them. For they mouth empty, boastful words and, by appealing to the lustful desires of sinful human nature, they entice people who are just escaping from those who live in error. They promise them freedom, while they themselves are slaves of depravity—for a man is a slave to whatever has mastered him. If they have escaped the corruption of the world by knowing our Lord and Savior Jesus Christ and are again entangled in it and overcome, they are worse off at the end than they were at the beginning.[89]

Isn't Scripture *fantastic*? In a few verses Peter brings together everything I have tried to share with you in this chapter. He reminds you not to wander off in the wrong direction like Balaam. You will be rebuked, and God will intervene. You then need to keep far way from people enticing you away from the new path you have taken. You want to be God-mastered and not sin-mastered. You must overcome and keep going, no matter how hard it may feel at times.

My prayer for anyone reading this book is that you will allow Jesus to intervene in your life and to become your daily guide as you walk in the wonderful hope of eternal life!

---

[89]   2 Peter 2:15–20.

Chapter 15

Bart—Blind but Full of Light

"**B**art, thanks for joining us on *BTL Live*," John says in a soothing voice. "I thought that we could tonight focus on the events leading up to your BTL act and the resistance you encountered."

Bart nods and begins to speak. His speech seems to have a sense of purpose about it. "Thanks, John. It would be my pleasure to tell you about my encounter with Jesus and the BTL experience of that day.

"I was begging in my usual spot along the road just outside the city of Jericho. Being blind made my existence very hard. Many nights I went hungry and cold. People avoided me, whispered about me, and were rude to me. I was considered something of a nuisance. I knew all the comings and goings of the city as I listened to what was said. That day I heard a large crowd approaching, and as they passed me by, people were talking about Jesus of Nazareth, saying that it was wonderful to follow and listen to Him. I decided there and then that I had to go BTL if I wanted to be healed by Jesus. So I began to shout, 'Jesus, Son of David, have mercy on me!'[90]

"Can I stop you there for just a moment?" John interjects. "There is a powerful message that I don't want us to miss. Sometimes to go BTL requires quick and obvious decisions. If you had kept quiet. Jesus would have passed you by."

"That's perfectly true," Bart responds. "I had to make sure that Jesus noticed me and did not pass by. The people in the crowd were getting irritated and kept telling me to keep quiet."

---

[90] Mark 10:47.

"It is rough to get open rebuke like that," John adds. "I think we all need to be careful about preventing people from coming to Jesus. Just prior to this, we, His disciples, had rebuked people from bringing their children for Jesus to touch. Jesus was not happy and said, 'Let the little children come to me, and do not hinder them, for the kingdom of God belongs to such as these. I tell you the truth, anyone who will not receive the kingdom of God like a little child will never enter it.'[91] We learned our lesson that day. It was not our role to judge who can come to Jesus or not."

Bart nods and continues. "The problem these people had was, now I was even more determined to ensure Jesus heard me, so I shouted even louder, 'Son of David, have mercy on me!'[92] I was determined to cross this line. It was so important that nothing or no one would stop me. This kind of positive attitude and drive is what is required if we are going to go BTL for Jesus.

"Then Jesus stopped. I had achieved my goal. I had His attention, and now He would come to me. But alas, no! He did the strangest thing. He asked the people to call me. I wasn't offered any help. Instead I was told to be happy and get up because Jesus wanted to see me. My joy could not be contained, and I jumped up. I then threw my trusty and necessary cloak aside. I knew that if I did not receive my sight, it would be difficult to find, but I believed that I would be healed. Nothing was going to dampen my enthusiasm to go BTL to Jesus.

"I fumbled my way to Jesus. Like some of you I found it tough going BTL. I eventually made it to Him, fully expecting Him to heal me. Then what seemed like an absurd question: 'What do you want me to do for you?' Jesus asked me.[93] What?! I was called *blind* Bart. I begged because I was *blind*. I fumbled my way to Jesus. Surely He could see that I was blind. After the initial shock wore off, I responded by asking to see.

"And Jesus' response?" John asks.

"'Go,' said Jesus, 'your faith has healed you.' Immediately I received my sight and followed Jesus along the road. Do you notice the difference now?" Bart asks.

---

[91] Mark 10:14–15.

[92] Mark 10:48.

[93] Mark 10:51.

"You are not emphasizing the physical ability to see," answers John, "but the more important aspect of sight. Sight that sees Jesus. I know that Jesus Himself emphasized this same point with Thomas, who did not believe that Jesus had risen, until he had seen Him. Then Jesus told him, 'Because you have seen me, you have believed; blessed are those who have not seen and yet have believed.'[94] This applies so clearly to your situation."

"It is about the faith to see the unseen. I had gone BTL with the attitude that Jesus *would* heal me and with enthusiasm." Bart replies.

"It says that you followed Jesus along the road. No mention of going back to get your cloak?" asks John

"But why go back to get that old worn and dirty cloak?" Bart asks rhetorically. "I had a new life, a new direction, and new clothes. As it says in Romans, 'Rather, clothe yourselves with the Lord Jesus Christ, and do not think about how to gratify the desires of the sinful nature.'[95] I had gone BTL to be clothed in Jesus."

"What made you so determined" John asks

Bart's eyes light up. "Ah! Now that is the key question. I knew that this line had to be crossed. It had to be crossed in faith and with a complete commitment. When we go BTL in moments that so obviously demand our action, it is essential not to look back. We need to step BTL with the full confidence that we are doing the will of God. This should be reflected in our attitude and determination."

"Bart, thanks so much for joining me today. You truly are an example of someone who stepped from darkness to light. You saw the line and went BTL without hesitation. Your example should inspire us all to take the next and the next step that takes us closer to Jesus. Finally, your willingness to persevere in the face of ridicule and rebuke is a reminder to all of us of the importance of spiritual growth."

Was That an Angel?

One of the many verses I enjoy in the Bible occurs in Hebrews. Its attraction is its mystery and intrigue. It says, "Keep on loving each other

---

[94] John 20:29.

[95] Romans 13:14.

as brothers. Do not forget to entertain strangers, for by so doing some people have entertained angels without knowing it."[96] I wonder how many angels I could have assisted. Could that beggar I ignored be an angel? You may find that you develop prejudices toward these desperate people. They become a nuisance and an irritation. In our minds and actions we judge them and rebuke them. This was not the way Jesus showed love. He wanted all people, including blind beggars and little children, to come to Him

An angel is after all a messenger of God. That means that you could fulfill this role. What message are you sending? Are you a messenger for the love and grace of God? The responsibility for us to encourage and support others on their spiritual journey is a key part of being a Christian. We have to engage with those around us, because, as every good messenger knows, you have two key aspects to the function. Imagine, if you will, that the FedEx messenger arrives at your door. He tells you he has no parcel or documents to give you and has realized that he is at the wrong house. You would be appalled at the service! You also are a messenger. You have a message. It's called the gospel! You have someone to give the message to: all who will listen. Beggars included!

John gives us a key message worth sharing. "This is the message you heard from the beginning: We should love one another."[97] The message centers on love. Love for your neighbor, and Jesus showed through a parable that your neighbor is anyone or everyone.

With this in mind, make every effort in the coming days, weeks, and years to be an angel carrying the message of love, and keep a lookout for that angel that you just may have missed the opportunity to interact with.

---

[96]   Hebrews 13:1-2.

[97]   1 John 3:11.

Chapter 16

Jairus — Converging BTLs

"You were a man of influence and religious standing at the time of Jesus. You needed to go BTL to save a life and two BTLs came together. Jairus, thanks so much for joining me. I believe that your BTL act has much to teach us about what we don't see when we go BTL. Please, could you share with us what brought you to Jesus and caused you to go BTL?"

Jairus responds in a quiet but confident voice. "Thanks, John. You are personally aware of most of the circumstances around my BTL act, but for the learning of others let me set the scene.

"I was a synagogue ruler, which at the time carried some prestige and responsibility. We followed the ways of the Law with fervor and rejected this man Jesus who claimed to be the Messiah. As a ruler I was expected to keep myself pure and undefiled by anything that would make me unclean. I tried to practice this as much as I could, given my circumstances. Let me not get ahead of myself. I will talk about that later."

"So what is it that caused you to go to Jesus?" John asks, looking a bit confused.

"Let me tell you, it was not easy to go BTL publically to the man that we did not even accept. But I had to. My twelve-year-old daughter was dying, and only one man could help. I humbled myself and fell at the feet of that despised man called Jesus and begged Him to come with me and heal my daughter."

"And what was His response?" John asks.

"He came with me," Jairus responds. No argument. No chastising. No rejection. No ridicule. What a powerful example to all of us. He knew that I had gone BTL out of necessity, but He accepts us no matter what has caused us to go BTL.

"Then *it* happened. God directed the paths of a few people to ensure that converging BTLs provided healing. The first was the physical healing. As Jesus was walking with me, a large crowd tried to keep as close as possible to Him. This meant a lot of pushing and shoving as people jostled for a position close to Jesus. In the middle of this chaos, a woman who had been suffering from bleeding for twelve years touched the edge of Jesus' garment. She had tried every physician she could find in search of healing, but with no success. Due to her bleeding she was unclean and alone. She loved her family, and they loved her. However, due to the laws from Leviticus 12 she was seen as unclean. She felt that the moment she touched Jesus' clothes, she was healed and He knew it too. 'At once Jesus realized that power had gone out from him. He turned around in the crowd and asked, "Who touched my clothes?" "You see the people crowding against you," his disciples answered, "and yet you can ask, 'Who touched me?'"[98] The disciples were shocked by the absurdity of the question, but Jesus would not let it go. It was not about humiliating the women but revealing the converging BTLs that God was orchestrating. Jesus kept looking and waiting until the woman came forward, trembling, fell at His feet, and revealed what had happened.

"I was shocked. I knew her. It was my wife! It was our daughter who lay sick and dying. Her bleeding had begun from the day she gave birth to her, twelve years earlier. It was a thing of constant pain and suffering for her both physically and emotionally. Take careful note of what Jesus said to her after healing her. 'He said to her, "Daughter, your faith has healed you. Go in peace and be freed from your suffering."'[99] She was not only healed. She was also set free from suffering—the suffering that comes from rejection and loneliness. Her decision to go BTL and to publically reveal it had converged with mine. Things were looking up. Next stop was our daughter being healed, but that's not the way God works.'

"That's so true!" John adds. "When things go well, we begin to expect God to behave in a way that is consistent with our view of the future."

---

[98]   Mark 5:30-31.

[99]   Mark 5:34.

"In our case, we learned that lesson very fast. No sooner had we rejoiced in the healing of my wife than we got the news that our daughter was dead. It was rough seas with huge ups and deep lows. We were, however, very blessed to have Jesus steadying the ship and guiding us. He was unmoved by the commotion around Him. First, He encouraged us to ignore the negative message and instead believe. Second, He thinned out the crowd to six of us. Finally, He got rid of all the wailing mourners, who laughed when He said she was just sleeping."

"Our Master has a way of making the toughest moments seem calm," John comments. "In your case He was arranging the circumstances so that you could focus all your efforts, thoughts, and prayers on your child."

Jairus acknowledges John's point with a nod and continues. "When Jesus took her by the hand and brought her back to life, we were amazed. Not only had he healed a child, but he had also reunited a family. Our independent BTL acts had been brought together in one harmonious result that we could not have dreamed possible."

"I am reminded of a scripture that highlights your point," John responds. "It speaks of God 'who is able to do immeasurably more than all we ask or imagine, according to his power that is at work within us.'[100] God will use His power to direct our paths. All He asks is that we go BTL, no matter how difficult or humiliating it may be. We cannot see or even comprehend what other BTL acts God has planned to converge with ours.

"So what other lessons did you draw out of your BTL act?" John queries.

"Well . . . ," says Jairus as he reflects on his answer. "I would also like to add that my own focus on protecting my status or career had meant that love and grace were absent. In a single afternoon Jesus showed me both!"

"Thanks, Jairus. What an amazing story of converging BTLs. We all need to remember that no matter how insignificant or individual our BTL acts feel, they may well form part of a bigger plan that God has for us and those around us."

---

[100] Ephesians 3:20.

Crossing Paths

You are at different times crossing paths with others as you perform your BTL acts. Sometimes before or during a BTL act you meet people also following their own BTL path. At the time the encounter may seem interesting but not significant. I am sure that in some cases you have personally experienced or known of situations where such "chance" encounters can result in amazing results. Don't ever underestimate these moments that God puts in your path. You know the moments I'm talking about: times when you feel the need to share some significant BTL act with a work colleague, a stranger on the bus, or a friend. If fear grips you in such moments, just remember that God is working with you every day, and the person you are sharing with also has a part in God's plan.

Consider the example of a man who happens to be traveling back to the city after a trip into the country. As he nears the city, he sees a large crowd and commotion along the road. He decides to take a closer look and makes his way to the front of the crowd. At first he can't see what is going on, but finally he sees a man near him. He looks in a bad way. He is about to ask who this is and what is going on when a strong, rough hand grabs him, and a military official shouts, "You! Get down there and help him carry that cross!" I am of course referring to the following verse in Scripture: "As they led him away, they seized Simon from Cyrene, who was on his way in from the country, and put the cross on him and *made him carry it behind Jesus.*"[101] Mark in his account of this event adds that Simon was the Father of Rufus and Alexander.[102] Rufus and his mother are mentioned in Romans by Paul as being of great help and support to him. It cannot be conclusively proved that this Rufus is the son of Simon, but I believe that the specific mention of Simon's sons is given for a reason. That day when Simon crossed paths with Jesus, his life changed forever. He too became a Christian and so did his family.

So always remember that, although your BTL act may not seem significant, it can be a tool by which more and more people choose to *take up their cross and follow Jesus*!

---

[101] Luke 23:26.

[102] Mark 15:21.

Chapter 17

Nicodemus — Hop, Skip and Jump!

"Nicodemus, it's so lovely to have you with me today. I know you don't particularly like big public displays, but I thought the stages of your BTL acts would be of great benefit to our readers. So if you don't mind," John asks politely, "would you please take us through your three BTL acts?"

"Good afternoon, John, and thank you for inviting me," Nicodemus responds with an air of formality. "Let me start with my first BTL act, but before I do that, it is worth remembering that all *my* BTL acts revolved around Jesus. The first was about finding Jesus. It was my first little BTL hop.

"I knew that Jesus must be from God, or else He would not be able to do the miracles He was doing. So I went out quietly one night to meet Him and understand more about His teachings."

"At night! Why at night?" asks John.

"I did tell you it was a *hop* of a BTL act. I was a person of prominence both in religious and monetary terms, and I was not that stage prepared to jeopardize that because of a meeting with Jesus," Nicodemus answers, sounding a little indignant.

He continues, "I told Jesus that I believed God was with Him, as we had all seen His miracles. I expected Him to respond to my comment. Instead He replied, 'I tell you the truth; no one can see the kingdom of God unless he is born again.'[103] I was confused. What was the relevance to my comment?

---

[103]   John 3:3.

"I decided to try to understand the reason for His reference to being born again. His statement was confusing. I wanted clarity. He responded with similar words but subtle yet important changes: 'I tell you the truth, no one can enter the kingdom of God unless he is born of water and the Spirit.'[104] His first answer to me was about *seeing* the kingdom of God. Now His emphasis was on *entering* the kingdom of God. To see God's kingdom I had to change my mind-set. I had to have a new vision of my future. To enter God's kingdom required action. Both are required as we walk toward God's kingdom. It was a huge and exciting lesson.

"He then said those now famous words: 'For God so loved the world that he gave his one and only Son, that whoever believes in him shall not perish but have eternal life.'[105] His message was both global and personal. I had sneaked in under cover of darkness to meet with Him. I needed to be bold and believe that eternal life came though Him. I was still afraid and not ready to reveal myself to those around me.

"Jesus' last words that evening really struck home: 'Whoever lives by the truth comes into the light, so that it may be seen plainly that what he has done has been done through God.'[106] It was a challenge to me. If I believed, then I needed to acknowledge publically and loudly that Jesus was the Son of God and the Messiah. No more late night meetings or hidden agendas. I needed to step into the light and make it clear where my allegiance lay."

Nicodemus pauses and adds, "I went home quietly and kept these things to myself."

"At times," John says, "it can feel overwhelming to go for a big BTL act immediately. I assume the things of that night played on your mind and led you to your next BTL act."

"That's for sure," Nicodemus responds quickly. "I had met Jesus in the beginning of His three-and-a-half-year ministry. My next BTL act was after He had really started to say and do more. I had kept a close eye on everything He was doing. A decision was made by the Sanhedrin to send the temple guards to arrest Him. They came back confessing the wonder of the things they had seen and heard. The rulers of the

---

[104] John 3:5.

[105] John 3:16.

[106] John 3:21.

Sanhedrin scolded the guards and said, 'Has any of the rulers or of the Pharisees believed in him? No! But this mob that knows nothing of the law—there is a curse on them.'[107] It was if God was prompting me. I believe that these kinds of situations happen so that we can make the next BTL act.

"Now I made a skip. More forward momentum but not quite there. I decided to take them on about their view that these simple folk did not understand the Law. I said, 'Does *our law* condemn anyone without first hearing him to find out what he is doing?'[108] Instead of prompting any type of discussion, this led to exactly the result I feared. They turned on me and accused me of being from Galilee and by inference a friend of Jesus."

"So what did you say?" John asks.

"I said nothing," says Nicodemus, casting his eyes to the ground. Looking up again, he continues, "I was afraid. I knew Jesus was the way of truth. I knew that Jesus was the Messiah. I was afraid and slipped back into the shadows where I would be unnoticed. I denied Him."

John decides to change the topic as he can see the pain that reliving this moment is causing Nicodemus. "So tell us about your final BTL act—or should we call this one a jump?"

Nicodemus seems to perk up and says, "By the time of Jesus' crucifixion, I knew I had to act both boldly and publically. I had heard Him say these words to the crowd and His disciples: 'If anyone would come after me, he must deny himself and take up his cross and follow me. For whoever wants to save his life will lose it, but whoever loses his life for me and for the gospel will save it.'[109] The evening of Jesus' death two secret followers *finally* went BTL. Joseph and I went to Pilate and got His body. We prepared it and laid it in the tomb. A disciple and religious leader both that night revealed that they followed Jesus. We stepped into the light. We did it in the full knowledge and faith that He would be raised. Why else would we finally jump?"

"Nicodemus, thanks so much for sharing your faith progression BTL. God made us wonderfully and uniquely different, which means

---

[107] John 7:46-48.
[108] John 7:51.
[109] Mark 8:34-35.

everyone's approach and path to going BTL is different. If nothing else, that is what we have shown with our interviews today."

With that John concludes the interview, gathers his papers, and leaves the room with Nicodemus.

The Long Jump

During my school years I always enjoyed sports. In particular I found fast-paced athletic events to be my favorites: the 100 meters, 200 meters, and long jump. I never could master the triple jump, however. The concept of hop, skip, and jump just did not translate into my actual actions. In most cases it came out as stumble, trip, and nosedive!

When preparing this chapter I was reminded of what a great metaphor for our BTL acts this is. Some of the people you have encountered so far have been world champion long jumpers. They see the line, charge up to it, and sail far beyond it. Some reluctantly run up to it and jump. Certainly not a world-record performance but still a jump. Some people stop at the line and get a shove to propel them over it. Others don't do the long jump at all; they prefer the triple jump.

You may be a triple jumper. It is not better or worse than the long jump. It's just a different way of eventually doing the same thing. It requires coordination but also, more important, progression. Those who, like Nicodemus, choose this path find it the most comfortable for them. You should never condemn or change the method they are using. They will jump in their time, not yours. Distracting triple jumpers during their different BTL acts can cause them to stop, falter, and ultimately fail to complete the jump.

So if you are a BTL long jumper, just remember that your way is not the best way, just a different way!

Chapter 18

Up Close and Personal

The interview room is now quiet and empty after John leaves the room with Nicodemus. Just then the editor of *BTL*, Guy Kieser, walks in. He is looking a bit nervous as he ensures that everything is just right in the room.

He starts talking. "The next guest is very special and will be hosted by a different interviewer." It appears that he is talking to himself. But then it happens . . .

Suddenly *you* are in the interview room with Guy. You are the special guest!

Guy greets you warmly and invites you to sit down. "As I was saying, we have a special interviewer for you. Take a seat, and make yourself comfortable. He will be here shortly." With that, Guy exits the room, closing the door behind him.

You sit in silence waiting to see who will interview you. The door creaks open slowly, and Jesus walks in. You jump to your feet out of a mixture of joy, surprise, and respect. He hugs you warmly and, motioning with His hand toward the chair, says, "Please sit down, my child. I have a few questions to ask you. What 'crazy' BTL steps have you taken in your life, and what motivated you to do it? If you never have, then what would cause you to do it?" (Remember Noah)

My answer to Jesus is . . .

"Are you, like Abraham, ready to act when God calls? What would prevent you from responding, and why?"

My answer to Jesus is . . .

"Are you open in your support of me among friends and at your place of work? What do you think those around you would say about you to me?" (Remember Daniel)

My answer to Jesus is . . .

"Have you felt that God is taking too long to respond and allow you to go BTL? What can you learn from Moses in regard to this?"

My answer to Jesus is . . .

"Do you judge others based on who they are rather than what they are doing in their BTL acts? If so, then make a list of people you need to get to know better and how." (Remember Rahab)

My answer to Jesus is . . .

"Do you feel inadequate to act and go BTL? Consider Gideon, and see how you can receive encouragement to trust in God."

My answer to Jesus is . . .

"What do you do when life seems overwhelming and the next BTL too much? What can Elijah teach us about dealing with this?"

My answer to Jesus is . . .

"How did David gain strength to face the giants in his life? Have you ever misread the signs, and what was the consequence of your action?"

My answer to Jesus is . . .

"Have you ever resisted a BTL act from God? If so, what was your logic in this course of action?" (Remember Jonah)

My answer to Jesus is . . .

"Think of times in your life when you should have acted but didn't. Do you find that you set expectations for God? How do you work with His schedule and not yours?" (Remember Esther)

My answer to Jesus is . . .

"Love is a strong and powerful emotion. What BTL acts have you undertaken for love? How could love be a motivator to go BTL?" (Remember Ruth)

My answer to Jesus is . . .

"Have you sometimes failed to go BTL? If so, how did you feel, and how do you overcome these feelings?" (Remember Peter)

My answer to Jesus is . . .

"How clear is your vision of me? Am I real and motivating enough in your darkest hours? Take some time to pray and read about me. How often should you commit to doing this?" (Remember Stephen)

My answer to Jesus is . . .

"Have interacting with me and believing in me changed you? How are you changed, and what should you still change?" (Remember Paul)

My answer to Jesus is . . .

"Have you ever gone blindly BTL, like Bart, and found the light beyond? If so, how does it make you feel to be in the light?"

My answer to Jesus is . . .

"Do you have examples in your life of converging BTLs like Jairus? What could have happened if you had not acted on your particular BTL?"

My answer to Jesus is . . .

"What expectations are you placing on yourself and those around you to go BTL? How do you prepare to go BTL?" (Remember Nicodemus)

My answer to Jesus is . . .

With every question, Jesus gives you an opportunity to reflect and learn from your answers. Some are easier than others.

You are amazed at how much you have learned from these men and women of faith.

Finally, Jesus says to you, "You need to keep looking for the line. It is there. I ask you to step over it, and I promise that you will never be alone before, during, or after you have crossed it."

Conclusion

We started off our time together discussing what courage and faith are. We took our first lesson from the *last verse* of Hebrews 10, where we learned that we should not be those who "shrink back" or avoid the line.

We then spent some time getting to know some amazing and faithful people in the Bible. I hope you have enjoyed getting to know these people better. Their lives have so many lessons to teach us and so many interesting nuances. Most of all, they are all real people facing real issues. They love, they fail, they try, they resist, but ultimately they go BTL. We saw how, like us, in times of crisis they hold out both hands. One is strong, firm, and full of faith. The other trembles, shakes, and is full of fear. Only when the two are clasped together in prayer can we make sense of our times of faith and fear.

We then spent time as Jesus interviewed *you*! I would encourage you to go though your answers to the questions in prayer with Jesus. Perhaps there are things you don't see that will be revealed.

After taking such a wonderful and exciting journey, where many of the examples come from Hebrews 11, I thought it best to end, the way Scripture intended, with the opening verses of Hebrews 12.

> Therefore, since we are surrounded by such a great cloud of witnesses, let us throw off everything that hinders and the sin that so easily entangles, and let us run with perseverance the race marked out for us. Let us fix our eyes on Jesus, the author and perfecter of our faith, who for the joy set before him endured the cross, scorning its shame, and sat down at the right hand of the throne of God.[110]

---

[110] Hebrews 12:1–2.

This fantastic passage brings together nicely what I have shared with you. Let me unpack it for you.

First, you *are* surrounded by a multitude of inspiring examples. You have looked of them for eighteen chapters. Yes, eighteen chapters! It includes you. There are examples today also.

Second, we are encouraged to "throw off" everything that holds us back. Do these words ring a bell? This is exactly what Bart did. He threw off that cloak to get to Jesus!

Third, we are asked to show perseverance. Think of Jonah, Moses, Stephen, Paul, and you. Note that it talks about a "race marked out for us" which implies a personal journey designed specifically for us. Steps with BTL acts that guide us toward Jesus.

Fourth, we are told to have vision. Jesus must be real in our lives. He should be our guide in our darkest hours. Peter confirmed to us that Jesus does have His hand outstretched.

Fifth, Jesus is called the author and perfecter of our faith. Did you know that Jesus is the author of several titles? The book of *life*,[111] the book of *salvation*,[112] and the book of *faith*.[113] He is the only person worth following. Through faith in Him, He offers salvation and life.

Sixth, we are given an insight into the way in which Jesus went BTL. His line was big, and scary. It was a line full of pain, mocking, blood, loneliness, and death. He knew it that night in Gethsemane. "Going a little farther, he fell with his face to the ground and prayed, 'My Father, if it is possible, may this cup be taken from me. Yet not as I will, but as you will.'"[114] He knew it had to be done and *chose* to step BTL for you and for me. But how? Well, Hebrews 12 reveals that He could see *beyond* the pain, *beyond* the mocking, *beyond* the denials, *beyond* the lies, *beyond* the death.

Jesus saw *joy* and because of it went *beyond* the line.

So what about you?

---

[111] Acts 3:15.

[112] Hebrews 2:10.

[113] Hebrews 12:2.

[114] Matthew 26:39.